ANTON MOSIMANN'S FISH CUISINE

Also by Anton Mosimann

Cuisine à la Carte
Cuisine Naturelle

ANTON MOSIMANN'S FISH CUISINE

MACMILLAN
LONDON

Acknowledgements

I would like to say thank you particularly to Dr Janet Gale, Lecturer in Health and Social Welfare at the Open University, to Lyn Hall, Chairman of La Petite Cuisine and Cuisine Creative, Kitty Adam, Kit Chan, Ralph Bürgin, Sylvia Baumann, Katrina Whone, Susan Fleming and Fiona Campbell.

A special thank you must go to the Kitchen Brigade of The Dorchester Hotel for their unstinting support, and to Tom Belshaw for his tremendous patience in working with me.

Designed by Robert Updegraff
Photographs by Tom Belshaw
Illustrations by Peter Bull

First published in 1988 by
MACMILLAN LONDON LIMITED
4 Little Essex Street London WC2R 3LF
and Basingstoke

Associated companies in Auckland, Delhi, Dublin, Gaborone, Hamburg, Harare, Hong Kong, Johannesburg, Kuala Lumpur, Lagos, Manzini, Melbourne, Mexico City, Nairobi, New York, Singapore and Tokyo

British Library Cataloguing in Publication Data
Mosimann, Anton
Anton Mosimann's fish cuisine.
1. Cookery (Fish)
I. Title
641.6'92   TX747

ISBN 0–333–45399–9

Typeset by Columns of Reading, Berkshire
Originated and printed by Golden Cup in Hong Kong
Bound by Hing Wah in Hong Kong

Contents

NOTE TO AUSTRALIAN READERS

Some fish used in the book are known by different names in Australia; the lists below indicate the European name and the common Australian name, or a substitute where the fish is not available.

European	Australian
Bonito	– Horse mackerel, bonito
Brill	– Flounder
Carp	– Barracuda
Monkfish	– Stargazer
Mullet	– Snapper
Perch	– Redfin
Sea bass	– Groper, coral trout
Turbot	– Flounder

To my mother

Introduction

When people ask me what I most like to eat – and to cook – my answer is always the same: fish. As a chef, I find buying, preparing, cooking and serving fish professionally satisfying, and as one who likes to eat good food I find that fish has no rival. It is a pure pleasure, and one that appeals to my senses at the same time as it takes care of my health.

I never fail to be inspired by the sight and feel of fresh fish on the slab. I enjoy the gleaming iridescence of the silver skin of a salmon, and the feel of the firm, pink flesh scented by the tang of the ocean. How can I cook this fish today, I wonder, as my mind runs through the fresh produce delivered that morning. Wherever I am in the world I am drawn to the stalls of the fish market. It is fascinating to see the range, shapes and sizes of the fish on offer: giant halibut and large black diamonds of turbot; streamlined mackerel with sharp snouts and pointed tails; fish from the lakes and rivers with muted colours and gentle stippling, and those from the southern tropical seas, ablaze with scarlet and yellow.

All through my life I have gathered memories and associations concerning this delicious food and I know that many of the small milestones of my personal and professional life have somehow been related to my interest in fish. As a young boy, I was already known in the village as a serious fisherman. Our house overlooked the blue waters of Lake Bienne, in the foothills of the Jura mountains in Switzerland. By the age of fourteen I had bought my own rowing boat and it was not uncommon for me to get up at four or five in the morning to fish in the still, deep waters of the lake. I still remember the sight and silence of the dawn, and me, alone in my boat, on that big lake. Any fear that I might have had when fishing in stormy conditions was never for myself but for my morning's catch. Later in my apprenticeship, when I was serving breakfast to fishermen, I was able to appreciate the hard work they had already accomplished. Because of my interest, and my experience as a teenager, I also understood more about the fish, how they had been caught, and the sort of conditions that they had had to endure before arriving in the kitchen.

It is not surprising that my travels in the Far East are closely associated in my mind with the fish there; I was greatly influenced by Japanese cooking during my year in that beautiful country. I love the utter simplicity and perfect style of Japanese cuisine. The choice and combinations of flavours in the sauces and marinades show a profound sensitivity to taste, and, although there is little on the plate, each dish is an expression of beauty. The preparation of *sashimi* (raw fish) in Japan is legendary – the fish is always exceptionally fresh, and simply prepared: sliced paper-thin, arranged with care, and served with a minimal amount of piquant sauce. Inspired by *sashimi*, I enjoy making similar dishes using British ingredients, like turbot tartar, and marinated salmon.

My preference for this simplicity and beauty, restraint and subtlety of flavour may result from my Swiss background; but it may also originate from my childhood memories of food scarcity: 'We only have a little to go round, but we shall prepare it beautifully. In this way we hope to make you happy.' Years later, it is still my aim to make cooking and eating, in this case fish, a joyful, happy experience.

I recall one occasion when travelling home from Singapore after a successful promotion of The Dorchester Hotel there, when my passion for fish over-ruled my senses: I was unable to resist the temptation of bringing back some exciting Far Eastern fish and, using a plastic bag filled with water, I carried the fish on to the plane to London. My two colleagues, who did not wish to be involved in explanations at Customs, followed me at a safe distance. I walked through, but they were stopped and searched! Such is my love of fish, and the extremes to which I will go to enjoy it!

I still like to learn and read about Oriental food and I was interested to read Cecilia Sun Yan Chiang's account of the 'boat dishes' of her childhood in China. These were prepared on sailing boats for moon-viewing parties, and the chef would cook on board fresh fish from the lake. Reading about this in the Far East reminded me of something that happened rather nearer home. Two years ago, I was a guest speaker at an international meeting on the prevention of heart disease. The meeting was in the north of Norway, 200 miles into the Arctic Circle. After a day of concentration, we all went on a boat trip around the fjord, and, as there were people fishing on the other side of the boat, I asked for a chef's apron and went down to the tiny galley below. The two young ladies there, not knowing that I knew something about cooking, were helpful and friendly! I believe it was a professor of psychiatry who landed a beautiful silver cod, which I cooked using the resources of the galley: barely simmering sea water, salt and vinegar. Freshness and simplicity of cooking made this one of the most delicious fish my colleagues had ever tasted.

Fishing on the Great Barrier Reef will long remain on my mind. I spent a week there with Peter Stafford, from whom I learned as much about food as I have learned from anyone. We fished in the sunshine as the wok warmed in the galley, and were able to enjoy a delicious parrot fish, a coral trout and other exotic treats minutes after the fish were landed. It was a marvellous experience to eat such delicacies.

Each fish has its own characteristics and subtlety of taste and texture. As far as cooking fish is concerned, it is this variety, and the countless methods of preparation, that attract me. The results that can be achieved with a few carefully selected ingredients are amazing: a culinary masterpiece can emerge from a really fresh fish with simply a little butter, a few herbs and some cream. The fish will not only be good to eat but should also be light to eat. There is hardly any other food which is so unpretentious in this respect.

Recently, we have become very conscious of the need for healthy eating, and we therefore value the nutritional qualities of fish, which contain important protein, vitamins and minerals. People are even beginning to think that extracts of some fish oils from the humble herring and sardine can help prevent heart disease. Fish is also easy to digest, has relatively few calories and thus fulfils today's need for light food. It has become a popular food and can now be seen enriching daily menus – and not just on Fridays. The local fish stall is now more popular than ever before, and supermarkets and delicatessens have installed fresh fish counters to meet this growing demand.

Whenever I am asked for a likely subject for a cookery course, fish is always high on my list. Many people are unsure of how to deal with fish, what to do about the scales, how to gut, skin and fillet. But more and more people want to learn. For that reason, this book contains notes and illustrations on how to prepare fish and shellfish, and notes, at the back of the book, about the fish I use. There is a section giving general advice on cooking fish and the recipe section and glossary also contain culinary facts and useful hints. The information in this book should help you to look more thoroughly at fish when buying it and then prepare and handle it with better understanding.

I have written this book in the first instance out of my love of fish as an ingredient, but also in response to many requests asking for new ideas for cooking fish, and how to prepare new or unusual fish. I have converted many conservative fish eaters to a *ceviche* or a delicate fish soup, and some have thereafter become dedicated fish lovers too. That is what I would like to achieve with this book. I hope that everyone who reads it will reach a better understanding of fish, and therefore become more familiar with it. I wish all fish enthusiasts and those who want to be converted, much pleasure in discovering, cooking and eating!

Bon appétit!

ANTON MOSIMANN
October 1987

Fish and Shellfish

'In the hands of a clever cook, fish is an inexhaustible source of enjoyment and taste,' said Brillat-Savarin, author of *The Physiology of Taste*. And this statement should be law in every kitchen, especially in those where the cook limits himself or herself to simple fish dishes with sauces. This nourishing and reasonably priced food offers so many variations that it would be possible to serve fish or shellfish daily for a whole year without repeating the same recipe twice. Not only that, but seafood requires only a minimum of preparation and cooking. 'If fish hadn't been around for thousands of years,' wrote one cookery expert, 'it would have had to be invented for today's hectic lifestyle.'

Fish

When cooking fish, you should be less concerned with the various zoological categories than with their quality and their suitability for certain types of dish. But it is important to recognise a few basic facts about the various types of fish, and the following should help.

In the most basic sense, fish are divided into two main groups – those from fresh water and those from salt water. However, there are several fish which live parts of their lives in both salt and fresh water – the sea trout and salmon, for instance. Fish are also further categorised by their shape, whether they are round or flat. Most freshwater fish are round – the trout for example – although the snake-like eel is in a class of its own. The flat fish – sole, brill, plaice, halibut, turbot, etc. – are all marine. The round versus flat distinction is important in a culinary sense in that a round fish will produce two fillets, a flat fish four fillets.

A further culinary significance lies in the nature of the flesh of the fish itself: whether it is oily, like mackerel and herring, or white and non-oily, like cod, sole, sea bass. White fish are also often described as either firm textured, like turbot or halibut, or soft textured, like herring and sardines. Fish can also be described as bony, like pike, carp – a category to which most freshwater and sea fish belong – but some fish are cartilaginous, with a skeleton formed of white cartilage rather than bone (shark, ray, monkfish etc). All these differences are included in the detailed descriptions beginning on page 237.

Flat fish deserve a separate mention because their 'evolution' is so interesting. All the flat fish are members of a single zoological order which chose at some point to be lazy and cunning, and to lie on their sides at the bottom of the sea waiting for their prey to come to *them*. As a result, they evolved into a flat shape, in order to camouflage themselves better on the sandy bottom, but the fry are still born 'round', with perfectly placed eyes on both sides of their heads. As they grow, though, one eye migrates over the top of the head to join the other, and the skeleton flattens. Both eyes remain on the mottled, darker side, while the side on which they lie is white. The fish which lie on their right sides and look left are called sinistral flat fish (the brill and turbot), while those that lie on their left sides and look right are called dextral flat fish, the majority of the remainder.

Shellfish

This is a collective but often confusing term for a rich variety of fascinating salt-water creatures that are not fish. The principal sub-divisions of this group are crustaceans and molluscs.

Crustaceans are those animals which have a hard, jointed external skeleton or shell. These include the various lobsters and lobster-like creatures, shrimps or prawns, and crabs. The only shellfish not to live in salt water is the tiny freshwater lobster, called ecrevisse, or freshwater crayfish, found for example in the chalk streams of England.

Molluscs can be further divided into three categories: the gastropods which are snail-like, with one shell (whelks and winkles); the bivalves, which have two shells hinged together and closed by strong muscles (oysters, mussels, scallops, clams, cockles); and the cephalopods, the most advanced of the molluscs, which are characterised by a distinct head with tentacles, well developed eyes and ink sacs (octopus, squid and cuttlefish).

Preserved Fish

Although fish or shellfish are most often eaten fresh, a number of fish are temporarily preserved in various ways – by salting and drying, smoking or pickling – and this would have been a necessity in the days before refrigeration. In medieval times people forced themselves to eat the heavily salted and highly spiced fish as their only source of protein; nowadays, choice smoked fish is the pride of a gourmet's table.

Britain has a rich heritage of smoking: herrings are smoked into bucklings, bloaters, kippers and sprats, and haddock into the renowned and respected Finnan Haddie and Glasgow Pales. One of the greatest delights of the table is smoked salmon, and my favourite is smoked Scottish salmon, lightly cured and smoked the traditional way in the East End of London; the delicate orange-coral flesh is almost transparent and the flavour inimitable. Other smoked fish, like smoked trout, eel, sturgeon and halibut all have their own individual flavours and undisputed place in the kitchen.

There are two types of smoking: cold smoking in pits or hot smoking in smokehouses over smouldering wood at a temperature of 80°F/30°C, or hot smoking in special ovens at 250°F/120°C, which cooks the fish. My first chalet was a converted farmhouse, the loft of which had been a smokehouse for three centuries; the walls had become encrusted with a rich ebony coating, the result of the fragrant smoke of oak, birch and Alpine herbs. Home hot smoking using a smoking box is becoming more popular, and particularly successful results can be achieved using oily fish like trout and mackerel and delicacies like scallops.

Perhaps the most famous salted and dried fish is the salt cod, or *bacalao*, which is transformed after a day's soaking in water into such famous dishes as *brandade de morue*. It is said that the Portuguese have more than 365 ways of cooking salt cod.

Herring is the fish most traditionally pickled, or 'soused', but we are also beginning to enjoy the Scandinavian pickled salmon, *gravlax*.

Fish Roes

Roe is the mass of eggs contained in a fine membrane in the female fish (hard roe), or the spawn of the male (soft roe or milt). From these a variety of fish delicacies are derived, principally that of caviar, of course. Fish roes are very nutritious.

Genuine caviar is the cleaned, slightly salted roe of the female sturgeon (of whose body weight, the mass of eggs can be up to 20 per cent). There are over a dozen species of sturgeon, and all are found in the northern hemisphere. Occasionally the fish are found fresh in fish markets, and they are also available smoked. However, it is their roe that is most valued, and for a long time Russia was the only producer, until in 1953 the Soviet Government presented Iran with certain fishing rights along the Caspian Sea. This sea and the Black Sea are the main centres of caviar production, although there is a Rumanian fishery at the mouth of the Danube. In France, a modest quantity of caviar was produced from sturgeon in the Gironde region (caviar, however, did not find its way properly into French kitchens until the 1920s when Russian immigrants reached Paris and Charles Ritz put it on the menu of his famous hotel). Some sturgeon are fished in America and caviar taken from them.

Nowadays most caviar comes from the Soviet Union, and is of varying quality. The best caviar is lightly salted and Russian tins are marked *'malassol'*, which comes from 'little' and 'salted'. Fresh, lightly salted caviar can be kept in the refrigerator at 2°C/36°F or, even better, 4°C/39°F for about a week. Caviar in a tin is semi-preserved and can therefore be kept at a normal temperature in the fridge for some time. Caviar should never look greasy or pulpy; it should not feel sticky, ooze liquid or taste sour. Once opened, a tin or container of caviar must be used immediately.

The eggs vary in size according to the size of the fish from which they are taken, and are named accordingly. *Beluga* is the caviar with the largest grains, coming from the largest sturgeon, which can be 3.6 metres (12 feet) in length, can live up to 100 years, and can contain 20kg (45lb) or upwards of eggs. This is the most popular caviar as well as the most expensive. Its granules are dark grey, firm and very fragile. *Ossetra* or *Osetr* caviar is particularly appreciated by connoisseurs. Its granules are somewhat smaller than those of the *Beluga*, and are coloured from yellowish to dark grey. It comes from a small sturgeon which can contain from 4–7.5kg (9–17lb) of eggs. *Sevruga* caviar is the smallest, with delicate eggs, dark grey in colour and very tasty. This is the most widely available. The fish can produce from 1.25–2.25kg (3–5lb) eggs. *Schlipp* caviar is less well known, and is a cross between *Sevruga* and *Ossetra*; the taste is similar to *Sevruga* and it resembles *Ossetra* in appearance. White caviar is something for élitists, very hard to acquire and therefore a curiosity. It comes from an albino sturgeon, has a very delicate taste, and is in fact my favourite.

Pressed sturgeon caviar is also available, and it is made from not quite mature or damaged eggs which are salted and then pressed. It takes 5kg (11lb) fresh caviar to yield 1kg (2.2lb) pressed caviar, and it is made up of several different types. As it is very concentrated, pressed caviar has a strong taste, and is suitable for garnishes or dishes where the appearance of the caviar does not matter so much – with, say, jacket potatoes or with small Jersey potatoes, on *blinis*, or as fillings in fish dishes.

Genuine caviar apart, there are many other caviars that would grace any menu or cold buffet. Red caviar or Keta is the roe of the Keta or dog salmon, which is found in Canadian and Siberian rivers flowing into the Pacific. It has very large translucent, coral granules, which are salted and preserved in glass jars. The roe from a river trout is often made into caviar too, and it is firmer in consistency, more amber in colour, and more delicate in flavour than Keta. It is much more difficult to obtain than Keta, although it can sometimes be bought frozen in Denmark and Germany.

Other 'caviars', known as German or Danish caviar, are made from the artificially coloured roe of the lumpfish, sea hare or sea owl, fished in the North Atlantic. The little black grains look like Sevruga but taste quite different. They can be used for decorative purposes in cold starters but the colouring may not be stable.

Many other roes are eaten, including cod, carp, herring, sole and mullet (which yields the Provence delicacy *Boutargue*, sometimes known as 'white caviar'), and I have enjoyed eating fresh shad roe on the East Coast of America.

Fish livers deserve a mention as yet another less known fish delicacy. The livers of whitefish, particularly the pollan, and of red mullet, codling, salmon and many other fish are much sought after. It is quite difficult to ease the livers from the fish, and it is therefore rare to find them available. It is possible to obtain excellent canned codling livers, but in order to find those from freshwater fish it is best to befriend a fisherman! Sea fish livers may be purchased occasionally in speciality fish shops. Fresh fish livers are best simply cooked by sweating them in hot butter, with or without shallots and herbs, for a very short while.

NUTRITIONAL VALUE

It is almost certain that fish was amongst the first food known to man. And nothing has changed in man's attitude to fish since then: it is as much in demand today as always, if not more so, its wealth of protein and lack of fat (particularly in freshwater fish) making it an ideal food for today's healthier diets.

Fish provides us with biologically high-value protein, with Vitamins A, B_6, B_{12}, nicotinic acid or niacin and pantothenic acid, other members of the B group. Fish also supplies minerals, giving us calcium, potassium, phosphorus and, in the case of sea fish, iodine and fluorine: 100g (4oz) cod fillet, for example, provides us with our daily requirement of iodine.

Most fish have a low fat content – useful for those on slimming diets – and even the oilier fish are valuable. Vitamin D is an essential only supplied by a limited number of foods, the major one of which is fish: cod liver oil is the greatest source (as it is of Vitamin A too), followed by oily fish such as herring, sardines, mackerel, eel, salmon and tuna. These oily fish also provide essential fatty acids which favourably influence the cholesterol content of our blood and protect us from heart disease. (These oils, in a lean white fish such as cod, collect in the liver.)

Fish is also light and easily digestible and is therefore often used as a constituent of special, invalid or infant diets.

Nutritional Value per 100g (4oz)
Edible Raw Flesh

	Kcal/kJ	Protein	Fat	Carbohydrates
Cod	79/331	13g	.3g	0
Turbot	87/363	8g	.8g	0
Salmon	208/869	13g	8.8g	0
Eel	285/1193	10g	17g	0

BUYING FISH AND SHELLFISH

It is well known that freshly caught fish taste best. There is simply nothing to compare with a brown trout caught in a crystal-clear mountain river and cooked a few hours later. Fresh, unfarmed salmon are highly prized. The Scottish season begins in February and is eagerly awaited by many; having leapt their way upstream, travelling sometimes for thousands of miles, the salmon's flesh is unmistakably taut and the flavour incomparable (though farmed salmon, while not of the same quality, does have its cheaper price and all-year-round availability to recommend it). But freshwater, unfarmed, fish are in fact a rarity on the fishmonger's slab and the ideal solution is to befriend a professional or an amateur fisherman – or take up the sport yourself.

When buying fish, the best thing to do is to go to your nearest wet fish or specialist shop or market and let yourself be advised by the experts there. Choose efficient, busy shops with a high turnover, or buy from the fish departments of supermarkets that, because of their regular customer demand, are able to offer a wide selection of fresh fish from a network of reliable suppliers.

In England, the main London fish market is closed from Saturday to Monday, so regard it as a good sign if you are not offered fish on a Sunday or Monday in a restaurant. Some fish and crustaceans are kept in tanks and are always freshly available – I myself keep a tank of live trout in my own kitchen at home.

Modern preservation methods, particularly the trawlers which freeze fish at sea (often gutting and filleting them as well), ensure that most types of fish are available throughout the year – even the more exotic ones that do not live within reach of our shores, or in our rivers and lakes. But the supply of fish and the species available depend on many things: the weather and the conditions at sea (storms and rivers in flood will stir up the sea bed and perhaps prevent the boats setting out), changes in warm and cold currents may produce indifferent fishing, and the cod war has given rise to reduced quotas. One should therefore understand if the choice of fish is sometimes limited, and appreciate the dangerous conditions that may be the cause.

The best tip is to experiment and find a good, reliable fishmonger whom you can trust, and buy from him regularly and enthusiastically.

It is useful to be familiar with the characteristics that signify really fresh fish. Some of the fish from the distant fishing grounds have been kept on ice for several days before the fishing vessel is able to bring them ashore and despatch them to the market.

	Fresh	Not fresh
SMELL	Light, pleasant and reminiscent of seaweed.	Unpleasantly fishy and strong, sour or mouldy.
GENERAL APPEARANCE	Shiny, slippery, moist, with a metallic shimmer.	Flat, colourless, dry, without iridescence.
SCALES	Strong, attached to skin, shiny.*	Loose, easy to remove or already partially off.
SKIN	Taut, deeply coloured, brilliant, adhering to fish.	Puckered, easily damaged.
EYES	Clear, protruding slightly, transparent.	Flat, glassy, opaque, opal-coloured, sunken.
GILLS	Moist, shiny, deep red or maroon.	Dry, greyish.
FLESH	Firm, translucent white or pink with a sheen.	Fish separates into large flakes, and is soft enough to retain the impression of a finger. Red or brown flecked. Fillets which are dry at the edges.

* Fresh, wild salmon may have missing scales from their leaps up rocky waterfalls on their way back to their birthplace.

Certain fish, such as trout or plaice, for example, are covered in a healthy slime when they are fresh. This should on no account be removed, although some retailers have taken to doing so in order to encourage customers to buy them. They should be avoided.

Fish should be taken home as soon as it is bought, and unpacked, scaled, gutted and filleted. Place in the refrigerator and use as soon as possible. If you want to keep it for a few hours, it could benefit from being placed between two sealed plastic bags full of ice. Skate should not, however, be cooked the day they are landed; they have a natural supply of urea, which gives off an ammoniac odour when really fresh and this needs a day or two to dissipate. Sole also benefits from a day or two in the refrigerator; when cooked absolutely fresh the flesh tends to be rubbery, and they are also very difficult to skin.

If at all possible I would advise you to try to avoid frozen fish. The process of freezing changes the internal structure of the fish – and rarely to its benefit; when the liquid in the fish freezes and the ice crystals expand, the cell walls break down, thus rendering frozen fish unsuitable for some recipes. In mousselines, for example, once the protein content of the fish is broken down, the necessary binding of the mousseline is difficult to achieve. Frozen fish is also more expensive.

The general rule to apply when buying frozen fish or freezing fish yourself is to use only the freshest fish: when buying frozen fish take care to buy fish that you know was frozen when absolutely fresh (this is difficult as no one can truly tell how fresh it was, and indeed whether it has been refrozen – you can only be as vigilant as possible). Don't freeze fish from the fishmonger unless you know it was caught that morning, and freeze it rapidly, at −28°C/−18°F. To thaw, remove the fish from the freezer in good time and let it thaw slowly, in its wrapping, in the refrigerator. Never 'thaw' fish in a bowl of water or under a tap.

Before cooking, fish should be rinsed quickly in cold water. The inside cavity should also be washed thoroughly and all traces of blood removed. Fish should never be soaked in water: the flesh absorbs the water immediately, which is detrimental to the cooking and affects the taste.

Choosing Fresh Shellfish

Crustaceans and bivalve molluscs should be alive (buy cooked shellfish only if absolutely necessary). Crabs and lobsters should be mobile – lively, even – and feel heavy in relation to their size. The tail of lobsters should spring back with a snap when straightened out. Both, if bought really fresh, can normally be kept alive for a couple of days by wrapping them in wet newspaper and storing in the refrigerator.

The bivalves should be firmly closed, the shells unbroken, or should snap tightly shut when tapped. If they do not, but gape open, they are dead and should not be bought. Cephalopods should shimmer on the fishmonger's slab.

In general, live crustaceans should be cooked or eaten as soon as they are bought, but some bivalve molluscs can be kept for a few days. Oysters, because they have sea water in their shells, can survive for about a week, if kept at a constant room temperature of 2–7°C/36–45°F, the deep shell beneath. However, the fresher the better, and worried oyster lovers can test by squeezing some lemon juice into the oyster when opened: as the acid drops on to the flesh, the oyster should react by 'wincing'.

How Much Fish To Buy

You can see from the following table how the wastage on fish varies, and with this, plus the further information below, you can work out the number of people a 'prepared', filleted fish will serve. Whole fish are usually sold with their entrails (which the fishmonger will remove on request), but fish from the North Sea are always gutted and sold without the head (which may be sold as well, if specially requested). For fish with very large heads, a little more per person must be allowed for.

Weight per Person to Buy

Fish	
Whole fish with large heads and heavy bones – John Dory, pike, sea bream, scorpion fish, monkfish, etc.	350–400g (12–14oz)
Whole fish with small heads – haddock, whiting, mackerel. This also applies to a tailpiece, eg cod, salmon.	300–350g (10–12oz)
Whole fish with small heads and light bones – trout, sardines, perch, herring.	250–300g (9–10oz)
Fillets	150–200g (5–7oz)

Percentages of Usable Fillets or Fish Meat

	Bones, skin and head	Fish fillets or fish meat
Cod	55%	45%
Monkfish	70%	30%
Whiting	45%	55%
Sole	50%	50%
Salmon	55%	45%
Pike	55%	45%
Turbot	50%	50%
Trout	40%	60%
Lobster (live)	75%	25%
Crab (live)	80%	20%
Shrimps (unpeeled)	60%	40%

CLEANING AND PREPARING

We spend more of our time *preparing* food for cooking than we spend actually *cooking*. It is the understanding, command and correct use of the basic methods of preparation that allow for the perfect accomplishment of the cooking process.

All the fish preparation processes can, of course, be done for you by the fishmonger, but it is worthwhile – and often necessary for certaintspec=al d=shes – to do it at home. The most vital piece of equipment is a slightly flexible and sharp filleting knife, with a blade of at least 15cm (6in) long.

Scaling Fish

Many varieties of fish have larger scales which must be removed before filleting (the knife will not be able to cut through the scales) and cooking (the scales will come off during cooking and spoil the dish).

Hold the fish by the tail, with a cloth so that you can keep a grip, then, using the blunt back of the knife, scrape along the skin away from you, towards the head of the fish. (Scallop shells are also good for scraping off scales, especially as they catch most of the flying scales.) Rinse well under cold running water – or, to avoid scales flying in all directions and sticking firmly to the walls, scale *under* the cold running water.

The fins can be cut off as well at this stage, especially those which are spiny.

Gutting Fish

Remove the head of a flat fish with two diagonal cuts towards the pectoral fins. The intestines will come away with the head. Rinse and pat dry.

Round fish can be gutted through the gills or belly. For the former, pull the gill flaps open and reach inside with a finger to hook out the gills and intestines. Rinse under a tap until the water runs clear (from the rear vent), and pat dry. To gut through the belly, cut from the gills to the rear vent and pull out the intestines (for large fish such as salmon use a spoon; for sardines use a pair of tweezers). Carefully remove any traces of blood, particularly along the backbone where there is a large blood vessel, rinse and pat dry. You could cut the head off too, if you like.

Preparing Shellfish

Crustaceans need little preparation other than cooking. Wash all bivalve molluscs well first, but do not leave them in water for too long otherwise this will impair their flavour.

Skinning Whole Round Fish

1 Loosen skin below head. Cut along backbone and along length of belly.

2 Draw off skin towards tail.

Skinning Round-Fish Fillets

Place skin side down and, using a sharp filleting knife, and short diagonal strokes, separate fillet from skin.

Skinning Whole or Filleted Flat Fish

With the exception of Dover sole, the dark skin only is removed from flat fish.

1 Cut through the skin above the tail.

2 Pull the skin up and back towards the head (a little salt on your fingers will ensure a good grip).

Filleting Flat Fish

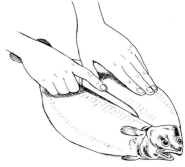

1 Cut off fins, and make incisions down length of backbone, and just below head.

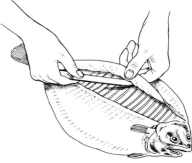

2 Slide knife under each fillet and cut until fillet is freed. Remove and repeat with remaining three fillets.

Filleting Round Fish

1 Cut along length of backbone and at an angle, behind the gills, on both sides of fish.

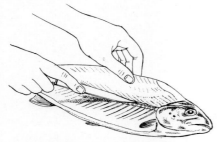

2 With clean, diagonal strokes, free and then cut away first fillet.

3 Lift off backbone.

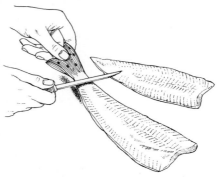

4 Cut off tail and remove small bones with tweezers.

Skinning Eel

1 Make cut in skin behind neck fins.

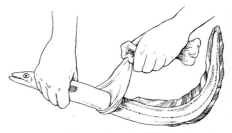

2 Loosen skin and pull off from head to tail. (You could attach head to a strong hook or nail, and pull skin *downwards*.)

Preparing Squid

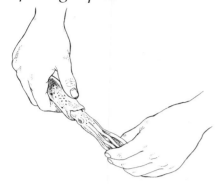

1 Gently pull apart head and body (intestines, beak and ink sac will come away with head: discard all but keep ink sac if you are using it).

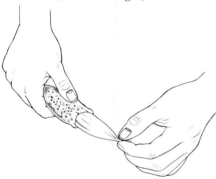

2 Remove transparent 'quill' and membrane from inside body sac.

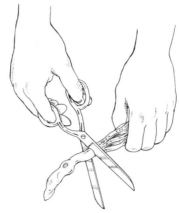

3 Cut off tentacles above head.

4 Skin body pouch. Remove and skin fins. Rinse all well. Body, tentacles and fins are now ready for use.

Extracting Cooked Lobster Meat

1 Twist off lobster claws and joints, and legs, and then split lobster in half.

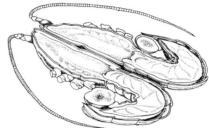

2 Scoop out body and tail meat, and coral.

3 Cut open claws and joints, and extract meat.

Preparing Mussels

Remove the beards, and scrub the shells clean, scraping off any barnacles. Place in clean water with a little salt for a couple of hours to help cleanse of sand. Throw away any that remain open.

Preparing and Opening Oysters

Place the oyster in a folded cloth on a firm surface, with the flatter shell upmost, hinged end towards you. Holding the oyster firmly in one hand, take an oyster knife or a short, strong blade in the other and insert the tip into the hinge. Twist to prise the shells slightly apart. Sever the muscle that holds the shells together, and remove the top shell, being careful not to spill the liquid in the lower shell. Cut the oyster loose from the lower, concave shell by running the knife around. If the oyster is gritty, rinse it in the liquid – never in water – which may then be strained through a muslin to remove any broken shell and grit and used in the recipe. Prepare clams in the same way.

Preparing Scallops

Hold in a cloth as for oysters, and then probe in with the top of a short, strong knife to sever the internal muscle. Heat on a hotplate or in a hot pan to open up the shells completely. Pull the shells apart, then, to free the scallop from the shell, run the knife under the brownish-grey outer rim of flesh (the 'skirt'). Separate the white muscle and coral from the other organs, and discard the latter and the skirt. Wash the shells and keep. Squeeze the coral to remove any black liquid.

Preparing Octopus

Cut off the tentacles, and then the top part of the body. The head, with the eyes, lies *between* body sac and tentacles and should be discarded. Turn the body sac inside out, and discard the intestines. Blanch in boiling water for 3 – 4 minutes and rub with salt to remove the skin. Cut the suckers off the tentacles and rinse all pieces well.

COOKING

Fish and shellfish constitute a very special category of meat. Fish flesh is composed of 70 per cent water, 20 per cent protein and 10 per cent fat. Fish muscle consists of segments of rather short fibres which are separated by large sheets of very thin connective tissue. There is very little connective tissue in fish – about 3 per cent of its weight, as opposed to 15 per cent in land animals – and what there is is very fragile. Because of this, and because the muscle fibres are short and their fat content relatively low, they generally should be cooked as little as possible, only to the point that the muscle proteins coagulate. Beyond this point, the flesh tends to dry out, losing its moisture content, its juices – and its taste – and will toughen or disintegrate. Overcooked shellfish become tough, dry and even stringy. The 'shrink temperature', the temperature at which the ordered structure of protein collapses, is about 60°C/140°F in meat, a mere 40°C/105°F in fish.

Therefore, in the simplest of terms, the delicate flesh of fish should never be cooked at too hot a temperature, nor overcooked. It is always best to cook fish only lightly.

Flat fish demand particular care in cooking: not only are they without natural oil or fat to baste the flesh naturally as it cooks, but their large surface area in relation to their thickness means that they lose their juices through evaporation, or into surrounding poaching liquor, more quickly than other fish.

The following sections offer helpful advice and instructions on the choice of which cooking method to use, and tips to make your fish cookery successful. Always season the fish well before applying any of these methods.

Grilling

Grilling is a healthy method of cooking any small- and medium-sized round or flat fish, and particularly for self-basting oily fish, such as mackerel and herring. It is also good for medium-sized fillets or portions; the juices are quickly sealed in and the cooking is light and quick.

Grilling tips
- Brush the grill rack or pan with oil to prevent sticking and, if you enjoy grilled or barbecued fish, invest in a double grill wire with a handle, which enables you to turn the fish over easily as it cooks.
- Do not overheat the grill; the fish will quickly dry out.
- If the fish is marinated, baste with the marinade during grilling, or baste with olive oil, to prevent drying out.

- If you like, you can form an attractive criss-cross pattern (*quadrillage*) on the fish, using red-hot skewers.
- The skin may be left on during grilling; the fat underneath will baste the fish, and the skin itself is delicious when crisp and brown.
- When grilling whole fish, slash the sides and rub with herbs and oil; this will allow the heat to penetrate to the deepest part of the fillet and the whole fish will cook more evenly.
- Once the fish has browned sufficiently, cover it loosely with aluminium foil to prevent drying out and charring.
- Most importantly, *watch* the fish cooking!

Poaching

Poaching is a traditional method of cooking fish; it is gentle and protective and helps retain the flavour, nutrients and texture of fish. It is particularly successful for whole or large pieces of fish such as salmon and, if used with caution, for flat fish.

Poaching tips
- Fish kettles are widely available for poaching whole fish, and whole turbot may be poached in a *turbotière*, a diamond-shaped copper pan. If you do not have a fish kettle with an easily removable insert, lay the fish on folded foil or muslin, allowing extra at each end for handles.
- The poaching stock should be heated to about 70°C /160°F, in other words, warm to the touch. It should never be allowed to bubble – if the stock boils, it will cause the fish to lose its natural moisture into the stock. The stock is traditionally reduced and used as the base for the sauce to accompany the fish.
- The fish should be completely immersed but not 'drowned' in the stock; it will be done when it has turned milky-white.
- Large whole fish should be placed in cool stock, and gradually heated to the required temperature; small fillets and *goujons* should be placed straight into the warmed stock (thus sealing the albumen and preventing loss of flavour).
- Fish to be cooked 'bleu' (see page 102) are poached in simmering stock for 5–10 minutes, depending on size.

Steaming

Steaming is an excellent and increasingly popular way of cooking small fish, fillets and portioned whole fish, especially delicate fish. The flesh will not dry out, and will remain juicy and firm. It is one of my favourite methods of cooking fish.

Steaming tips

- Spread the metal basket or perforated pan insert with butter or aluminium foil and place the fish in it in a single layer to enable the hot steam to circulate evenly and freely.
- If you wish to give more flavour to the fish, place it on a bed of seaweed or herb trimmings.
- The stock beneath the basket or insert will reduce; take care never to let it boil away, and add more boiling stock if necessary. It will be an ideal base for a sauce.

Sautéing

Sautéing is a gentle, flavour-enhancing method of cooking fish particularly suitable for small fish or fish fillets with delicate or mild flavours.

Sautéing tips

- Dry the fish well on kitchen towel before sautéing.
- A small amount of fat should be used, preferably unsalted, clarified butter, which can withstand much higher temperatures without burning than unclarified butter. If you like, you can use equal quantities of clarified butter and groundnut oil.
- Use a wide, shallow pan to enable you to turn over the fish without breaking it; and do not overcrowd it.
- The fish may be floured first – keep a container of flour seasoned with salt and pepper for this purpose. The secret of flouring is to dry the fish, flour it generously and then brush most of it off so that only a very fine dusting remains: it will cook to a tasty golden brown crust in the hot fat.
- Sautéed fish should be thoroughly drained on kitchen towel before serving, and not covered.

Braising

In this method of cooking, the fish is usually moistened with a little liquid (wine, stock, champagne) and cooked in a medium oven on a bed of softened, finely sliced aromatic vegetables. It is generally used for whole fish such as salmon, bream or turbot, and for portioned fish or large tail pieces.

Braising tips

- If the fish is not covered, baste it regularly with the cooking juices to prevent it drying out.
- The skin of whole fish should be scored so that flavours and stock can penetrate the flesh.
- The stock will reduce slightly during braising, and it can then be used for the sauce.
- Sliced, par-boiled potatoes may be cooked in the same pan, and these will be flavoured by the mingled juices of the fish and the sauce.

Deep-frying

Deep-frying is most suited to tiny whole fish, such as whitebait, small fillets or goujons of white fish such as perch, and to squid and small shellfish such as prawns.

Deep-frying tips

- The pieces of fish should be of the same size, and cut quite small or they will brown too much before they are cooked through.
- Use clear, fresh oil, with no aftertaste. Groundnut oil provides a good frying medium, although it is traditional to use a hard fat in some parts of the country. (Some deep fryers are designed to take oil only.)
- The tender flesh of the fish is best protected from the heat and oil by a covering of flour, breadcrumbs or batter.
- To obtain good, crisp results, always fry fish in two stages: blanch first at about 160°C/325°F, and then refry at 190°C/375°F.
- Fry the fish in batches, and don't overcrowd the pan.
- The oil must be hot enough to turn the liquid in the fish into steam; the escaping steam prevents the oil from penetrating the fish.
- Smoked fish should not be fried unless it is in batter, and avoid salting the fish near the fryer: both practices will cause the oil to break down and smoke.
- Excess fat should be removed by draining the fish on kitchen towel.
- Deep-fried fish must be served immediately and should not be covered or reheated.

Stewing

Stewing is a similar process to simmering, and may take place either in the oven or on top of the cooker. Use firm, boned fish, like monkfish, cod or eel. It is an excellent method of cooking octopus.

Stewing tips

- The pieces of fish should be as near as possible of equal size.
- The casserole should have a well-fitting lid.
- A slow heat should be maintained throughout the cooking.
- Add extra stock if the stew becomes too dry.

Baking and roasting

Baking and roasting are fairly similar processes in fish cooking, and are best suited to large, whole fish or thick, large fish fillets.

Baking and roasting tips

- Large fish may be boned and stuffed, and this is a quick, easy way to serve fish for a large number of people. Sew the cavity with dark thread before baking; the thread can be easily removed when the fish is done.
- If baking, baste the fish with a little stock or wine; use olive oil or butter if you are roasting.
- Small fillets of fish are delicious served *en papillote* (see page 233); this is one of the most simple and effective methods of cooking fish, as it involves little preparation and no flavour is lost.

Fish Cooked in its own Juices

I include this method of cooking fish separately because it is a relatively new method of cooking that does not easily fit into one of the above categories. It is particularly suitable for small whole fish such as mullet or for fillets and steaks, such as salmon.

A stainless steel or non-stick pan with a specially made base and hermetically sealed lid is essential (some pans also have lids with thermometers, making exact temperature control possible). Place the fish in the cold pan, without fat or liquid, and it will cook in its own juice on the lowest heat. The fish will retain its own flavour and will not fall apart; it will also have no added calories. You can add herbs if you wish.

How to Tell when Fish is Done

'Cook with feeling' is the advice I give to all my young chefs; this is the best guide to cooking times. I have been cooking since I was seven years old, and I have learned to use all my senses; when cooking fish, however, the sense of touch is particularly valuable.

The flesh of raw fish will feel soft and spongy in varying degrees; cooked fish feels tender and offers a little resistance; and overcooked fish is hard, rubbery, and breaks cleanly. By pressing the thickest part of the fish you will soon begin to recognise the change brought about by the cooking process. In general, the length of time fish takes to cook is governed by the thickness of the fillet, or the whole fish, never by the actual length of the fish.

Other signs are:

- The flesh turns from translucent to opaque; it should be juicy and barely opaque when the fish is taken off the heat (the fish will continue to cook as the dish is finished and served). To test, with the tip of a knife neatly flake a little of the fish in the deepest part of the fillet; you can conceal your test with the garnish or a little sauce.
- With whole fish, such as sea bass and trout, the dorsal fin will pull out easily when the fish is cooked.
- If you are cooking a terrine, insert a skewer in the middle, hold it there for a second, and place it against the inside of your wrist. The skewer should feel hot, but not searingly so.

BASICS

Fish Stock

FOND DE POISSON

To produce a very fine quality fish stock, use the bones of good, fresh white fish such as sole and turbot.

Makes 1 litre (1¾ pints)

1kg (2¼lb)	broken-up white fish bones and trimmings
50g (2oz)	white mirepoix (onions, white of leek, celeriac, fennel leaves, dill)
30g (1oz)	mushroom trimmings
20g (¾oz)	butter
100ml (4fl oz)	dry white wine
1.2 litres (2 pints)	water
	salt, freshly ground pepper

- Thoroughly wash the fish bones and trimmings.

- In a large saucepan, sweat the mirepoix and the mushroom trimmings in the butter.

- Add the fish bones and trimmings, white wine and water and simmer for 20 minutes, occasionally skimming and removing the fat.

- Strain through a muslin or a fine sieve and season with salt and pepper.

Mussel Stock

FOND DE MOULES

Makes 1 litre (1¾ pints)

1.5kg (3½lb)	mussels, soaked, scrubbed and thoroughly cleaned, beards removed
80ml (3fl oz)	water
80ml (3fl oz)	dry white wine
1	small shallot, finely chopped
10g (½oz)	celery, diced
	a few sprigs of parsley
	a little thyme
	freshly ground pepper

- Discard any mussels that are broken or that float or remain open during cleaning.

- Bring the water, wine, shallot, celery, parsley and thyme to the boil in a wide, shallow pan.

- Add the mussels and season with pepper. Cover and allow to boil for 3–4 minutes (only until the mussels open, or they will become tough).

- Remove the mussels from the stock with a sieve or skimming ladle and use elsewhere when needed. (Discard any that have not opened.)

- Leave the stock to stand for 3–4 minutes to allow any particles to settle, and then strain carefully through a fine muslin so that no sand remains in it.

Court Bouillon

This stock is used for poaching fish and for boiling lobster and shellfish, etc.

Makes 2.5 litres (4¼ pints)

500ml (*16fl oz*)	dry white wine
2 litres (*3½ pints*)	water
200g (*7oz*)	carrots, peeled and diced
100g (*4oz*)	white of leek, diced
100g (*4oz*)	onions, diced
50g (*2oz*)	celery, diced
1	clove of garlic, unpeeled
5	sprigs of parsley
1	small sprig of thyme
½	bay leaf
5	white peppercorns, crushed
3	coriander seeds
	salt

- In a large saucepan, bring the white wine and the water to the boil.

- Add all the remaining ingredients, except for the salt, and allow to simmer for 10 minutes. Season with salt and then strain through a fine sieve.

White Poultry Stock

FOND BLANC DE VOLAILLE

The boiling fowl used to make this stock can be used afterwards for various cold dishes.

Makes 1 litre (1¾ pints)

1	boiling fowl (or 900g (2lb) poultry bones and trimmings), blanched for 2 minutes
3 litres (5¼ pints)	water
50g (2oz)	white bouquet garni (onion, white of leek, celeriac and herbs)
	salt, freshly ground pepper

- Put the boiling fowl or poultry bones and trimmings in a large saucepan, fill up with the cold water, bring to the boil and skim.

- Add the bouquet garni and seasoning.

- Leave to simmer carefully for 2 hours, occasionally skimming and removing the fat.

- Strain the stock through a muslin or a sieve and season to taste.

Lobster Butter

BEURRE DE HOMARD

Lobster butter enriches and imparts a special flavour and colour to sauces to be served with fish. You can make crayfish butter in the same way, using crayfish shells (as red as possible) instead of lobster shells.

    The butter will keep in the refrigerator for up to 10 days, and will also freeze well.

100g (4oz)	lobster shells, chopped
150g (5½oz)	butter
	a little brandy
	salt, freshly ground pepper

- Roast the lobster shells on a baking tray in a moderate oven (180°C/350°F/Gas 4) for about 15 minutes (this enhances and intensifies the lobster flavour).

- Crush the shells between sheets of greaseproof paper with a rolling pin until quite fine, and beat into the butter. Place the butter in a saucepan and stir constantly with a wooden spoon over a gentle heat until the butter is clarified, skimming occasionally.

- Fill up the saucepan with water, and strain the liquid into a bowl. Set aside in a cool place. In a few hours the butter will have separated from the water and can be easily removed. Discard the water.

- Put the butter in a saucepan and heat it to simmering point. Season with salt and pepper, add the brandy and strain through fine muslin into a bowl. Cover and refrigerate until needed.

Fish Sabayon

SABAYON DE POISSON

SERVES 4

1 tablespoon	Noilly Prat
1 tablespoon	dry white wine
1	small shallot, finely chopped
2	egg yolks
50g (2oz)	butter, chilled and cut into cubes
	the juice of half a lemon
	salt, freshly ground pepper
	cayenne pepper

- In a saucepan, combine the Noilly Prat and white wine with the shallot and reduce by half.

- Transfer to a stainless steel or a glass bowl and stir in the egg yolks. Beat the mixture with a balloon whisk over a pan of simmering water until it is thick and the whisk leaves traces (the 'ribbon stage').

- Remove the bowl from the heat and whisk in the butter, piece by piece.

- Strain through a fine sieve or a muslin and then bring back to the boil.

- Season to taste with salt, pepper, cayenne and lemon juice, and serve.

White Wine Sauce

SAUCE AU VIN BLANC

This is a modern white wine sauce, and it may be used as a base for many variations.

Once the cream has been added simmer the sauce gently or the flavour may be spoiled.

You can use cornflour mixed with a little cold water to thicken the sauce, instead of butter, if you prefer.

SERVES 4

200ml (*7fl oz*)	fish stock (see page 22)
100ml (*4fl oz*)	dry white wine
50ml (*2fl oz*)	Noilly Prat
1	small shallot, finely chopped
150ml (*¼ pint*)	double cream
50g (*2oz*)	butter, chilled and cut into cubes
	salt, freshly ground pepper

- In a large saucepan combine the fish stock, white wine, Noilly Prat and shallot and reduce by half by fast boiling.

- Add the cream and boil gently to reduce to the required consistency.

- Remove the pan from the heat and whisk in the butter cubes, piece by piece. Strain the sauce through a fine sieve or a muslin and bring back to the boil. Season to taste with salt and pepper and serve.

White Wine Sauce with Caviar

SAUCE MOSCOVITE

Make a white wine sauce (see above) and carefully stir in 30g (*1oz*) caviar. Check seasoning.

White Wine Sauce with Whipped Cream

SAUCE MOUSSELINE

Make a white wine sauce (see above) and stir in 50ml (*2fl oz*) whipped cream. Season to taste.

Saffron Sauce

SAUCE AU SAFRAN

Saffron is a delicate spice. Store it away from the light and add it at the end of cooking or you may cook out the flavour completely.

SERVES 4

200ml (*7fl oz*)	fish stock (see page 22)
100ml (*4fl oz*)	dry white wine
75ml (*3fl oz*)	Noilly Prat
1	small shallot, finely chopped
175ml (*6fl oz*)	double cream
	a few strands of saffron
25g (*1oz*)	butter, chilled and cut into cubes
	salt, freshly ground pepper
	cayenne pepper

- In a saucepan, bring the fish stock, white wine, Noilly Prat and the shallot to the boil and reduce rapidly until only 100ml (*4fl oz*) remains.

- Add the cream and bring back to the boil. Reduce again gently until the sauce is thick enough to coat the back of a spoon.

- Remove the pan from the heat, add the saffron strands and allow to infuse for a few minutes.

- Still with the pan off the heat, whisk in the butter a little at a time. Strain the sauce through a muslin or a fine sieve and then bring back to the boil.

- Season to taste and serve.

Herb Sauce

SAUCE AUX HERBES

If all the herbs are not available, use more of one or the other. Cut the basil last as the leaves blacken if prepared in advance.

SERVES 4

150ml (¼ *pint*)	fish stock (see page 22)
100ml (*4fl oz*)	dry white wine
50ml (*2fl oz*)	Noilly Prat
1	small shallot, finely chopped
150ml (¼ *pint*)	double cream
1 teaspoon	chervil, finely snipped ⎱ keep stalks
1 teaspoon	dill, finely cut ⎰
50g (*2oz*)	butter, chilled and cut into small cubes
1 teaspoon	basil, finely cut
1 teaspoon	chives, finely cut
	salt, freshly ground pepper

- Place the fish stock, white wine, Noilly Prat and the shallot in a pan and reduce until 100ml (*4fl oz*) remains.

- Add the cream and bring back to the boil. Crush the chervil and dill stalks lightly and add to the sauce.

- Simmer until the sauce is thick enough to coat the back of a spoon. Pass though a fine sieve or a muslin.

- With the pan off the heat whisk in the butter, a little at a time. Add the herbs, bring back to the boil, season to taste and serve.

Red Pepper Sauce

SAUCE AUX POIVRONS ROUGES

SERVES 4

2	medium red peppers, deseeded and cut into pieces
1 tablespoon	olive oil
2	small cloves of garlic, unpeeled and crushed
1	small shallot, sliced
2	sprigs of thyme
600ml (*21fl oz*)	fish stock (see page 22)
100ml (*4fl oz*)	double cream
	salt, freshly ground pepper and a little sugar to taste

- Heat the olive oil in a heavy saucepan, and sweat the garlic and the shallot until transparent.

- Add the pieces of pepper, the thyme and the fish stock, season and bring to the boil. Simmer for about 15 minutes, stirring occasionally, until the peppers are tender.

- Liquidise the mixture until smooth, stir in the cream, reheat and adjust the seasoning with salt, pepper and sugar to taste.

Yellow Pepper Sauce/Green Pepper Sauce

Follow the recipe exactly as for red pepper sauce (above) but substitute yellow and green peppers as appropriate. You can make the green pepper sauce a brighter green by adding a few spinach leaves.

Hollandaise Sauce

SAUCE HOLLANDAISE

Hollandaise sauce flavoured with tarragon is also delicious with fish; simply replace the white wine vinegar with tarragon vinegar.

SERVES 4

1 tablespoon	white wine vinegar
1	small shallot, finely chopped
2–3	white peppercorns, crushed
1 tablespoon	cold water
3	egg yolks
200g (7oz)	butter, melted and clarified
	a little lemon juice
	salt, freshly ground pepper

- Combine in a small saucepan the vinegar, shallot and peppercorns, and boil until the vinegar is almost completely reduced. Transfer the reduced vinegar mixture to a basin and add the cold water and then the egg yolks and, over a pan of gently simmering water, whisk into a thick, foamy binding cream.

- Remove the bowl from the pan of water and very gradually whisk in the butter.

- Season the sauce to taste with salt, pepper and lemon juice and then strain through a muslin or a fine sieve and use as required.

  Note The pan of water under the bowl of sauce must be barely simmering; if the sauce overheats it will separate. If this does happen, quickly whisk in a little cold water – the sauce should once again become smooth and creamy.

Lobster Sauce

SAUCE DE HOMARD

SERVES 4

1	live female lobster, weighing about 450g (*1lb*)
50g (*2oz*)	butter, softened
2 tablespoons	olive oil
50g (*2oz*)	mirepoix (made of carrots, onions, leek, celeriac and parsley)
50g (*2oz*)	tomatoes, diced
2 tablespoons	brandy
100ml (*4fl oz*)	dry white wine
500ml (*16fl oz*)	fish stock (see page 22)
½ tablespoon	dill, finely cut
½ tablespoon	tarragon, finely snipped
	a little fish glaze (see below)
	salt, freshly ground pepper

- Splash the lobster with cold water and plunge into a large pan of boiling water for 1 minute to kill it. Remove from the pan and cut the body in half lengthwise; then chop it into pieces (leave the shell on); remove and discard the stomach. Blend the coral with the butter and chill.

- Heat the olive oil in a heavy saucepan, add the lobster pieces and the claws and, using a wooden spatula, sauté on all sides until the shell is completely red.

- Add the mirepoix and tomatoes and sweat well for a further 2–3 minutes.

- Sprinkle over the brandy and flame it; then add the wine, fish stock and herbs. Bring to the boil.

- Remove the lobster pieces and take the meat from the shell (use the lobster meat in another recipe). Crush the lobster shell as finely as possible and return to the stock. Simmer for approximately 30 minutes on a low heat.

- Add the fish glaze and reduce the stock to one third of its original volume. Whisk in the butter-and-coral mixture little by little, to thicken the sauce.

- Strain the sauce through muslin and season to taste.

Fish Glaze (makes 200ml (*7fl oz*))

Take 5 litres (*8¾ pints*) fish stock (page 22) and, in your largest saucepan, simmer it until it has reduced considerably. Pour the reduced stock into a smaller pan and continue to simmer and reduce.
As the stock reduces, keep transferring into smaller saucepans. Keep the edges of the pan clean and clear with a flexible spatula.
Simmer until about 200ml (*7fl oz*) remain. Cool and store in the refrigerator.

Tomato Coulis

SAUCE COULIS DE TOMATES

The colour of this sauce depends on the bright red colour of the tomatoes; to guarantee ripeness, buy them a few days in advance.

SERVES 4

550g (1¼lb)	firm, ripe tomatoes, blanched, skinned, deseeded and chopped
20g (¾oz)	butter
2	small shallots, finely chopped
½	clove of garlic, crushed
1	sprig of thyme
1	sprig of rosemary
	salt, freshly ground pepper and a little sugar

- Sauté the shallots and garlic with the butter in a saucepan for 3–4 minutes until transparent.

- Add the herbs and sauté very gently for a minute more. Add the tomatoes and simmer for 10–12 minutes.

- Remove the herbs and purée the tomatoes in a blender.

- Put the sauce back into the saucepan, bring to the boil, and season with salt, pepper and sugar to taste.

Puff Pastry

PÂTE FEUILLETÉE

The crisp, melt-in-the-mouth quality of pastry offers a delicious contrast to the tenderness of fish.

SERVES 4

450g (*1lb*)	strong plain white flour, sieved
175ml (*6fl oz*)	water
15g (*½oz*)	salt
500g (*1lb 2oz*)	butter
	flour for dusting

- Combine in a bowl the flour, water and salt, and mix well. Knead to a smooth paste. Allow to rest for 30 minutes.

- Roll out the paste to a square about 2cm (*¾in*) thick.

- Press the butter until fairly flat and place in the middle of the paste. Fold the edges of the paste over the butter so that it is completely enclosed in it.

- Roll the paste and butter into a long rectangle 2cm (*¾in*) thick.

- Fold the two ends of the paste evenly towards the centre so that they meet in the middle of the paste. Then fold over both halves of the paste so that the middle now becomes one of the sides. This is one double turn. Rest in the refrigerator for 20 minutes.

- Roll the paste and butter into a rectangle, lay one third of the paste over the middle third and cover this part with the other third so that the paste, which is 2–3cm (*¾–1¼in*) thick, is in 3 layers (this is called a single turn).

- Puff pastry requires 4 double turns or 6 single turns. Between each turn the paste should rest for 20 minutes in a cool place. For pastry cases one more double or single turn should be made. The pastry should rest for at least 2 hours before use so that it can be rolled out regularly; it must be firm and a sharp knife should be used to make a clean cut. This can, of course, also be done with a pastry cutter.

Note As can be seen from the above recipe, the 'turns' in the making of puff pastry are to produce layers of butter between layers of paste. Butter contains 60 per cent water, which is converted to steam during baking; it is the steam 'pillows' created that cause the pastry to rise.

The pastry should be kept cold during handling: if it becomes too warm the butter will melt and seep through the layers of paste, so it is important to let the pastry cool and rest between turns. When cutting and shaping the pastry it is often useful to firm it up for a while in the freezer before handling.

Filo Pastry

Makes 650g (1¼–1½lb)

300g (*11oz*)	strong plain white flour
100g (*4oz*)	cornflour
½ teaspoon	salt
250ml (*8fl oz*)	water
	flour for dusting

- Sieve the flour, cornflour and salt together into a bowl. Make a well in the centre.

- Put about half the water into the well, and gradually draw the flour into the water, mixing smoothly and evenly. Add the remaining water and mix until the dough is smooth and does not stick to the hands.

- Cover the dough with a damp cloth and leave to rest for 1–2 hours in a cool place. This allows it to soften and become elastic, which is essential for rolling it out.

- Cut the dough into quarters, and cover the pieces not being rolled with an upturned hot bowl (this helps to warm the dough and make it pliable). Start rolling one piece out, gradually making the sheet thinner and thinner (use plenty of flour).

- If the dough sheet becomes too large and unwieldy, cut in half and continue to roll. When as thin as possible by rolling, place the sheet over the back of the hand, and pull gently down from the edges to stretch even more. Work carefully so that it does not break.

- Roll other pieces of dough in the same way, and cover dough and sheets at all times with a sheet of plastic or cling film. Use sheets as quickly as possible.

Home-made Egg Noodles

NOUILLES AUX OEUFS FRAIS

The consistency of the dough can depend on the size of the egg; if you use a large egg, add a little more flour to achieve a firm, manageable dough.

SERVES 4

200g (*7oz*)	strong plain white flour (or fine wholewheat flour), sieved
25g (*1oz*)	fine semolina
½ tablespoon	olive oil
1	egg
	a pinch of salt
3–4 tablespoons	hot water
	flour for dusting

- Mix the flour and semolina together in a large bowl and make a well in the centre. Place the other ingredients in the well. Gradually work the flour and semolina in towards the middle and knead into a very firm, smooth dough.

- Wrap in a damp cloth and allow to rest in a cool place for at least 2–3 hours.

- Divide the dough into five pieces and roll out each piece as thinly as possible. Lay the pieces on top of each other and cut into strips approximately 6mm (¼in) wide. An alternative method of cutting is to roll the five pieces of dough into thin circles. Fold each circle in loosely from both sides, parallel to the middle. Do this again until both folded edges meet in the middle. Then cut the dough crosswise into strips. (You can of course use a pasta machine for this.)

- These noodles may be cooked when fresh or left to dry out. Boil for 2–3 minutes if fresh, and for about double that time if dried.

Note If wholewheat flour is used instead of plain the pasta will be brown rather than white and will render a stiff dough.

Home-made Saffron Noodles

NOUILLES AU SAFRAN

The warmth in colour of these golden noodles will illuminate a white fish when served as an accompaniment.

SERVES 4

200g (7oz)	strong plain white flour, sieved
25g (1oz)	fine semolina
½ tablespoon	olive oil
1	egg
	a pinch of salt
	a few strands of saffron or a pinch of saffron powder
3–4 tablespoons	hot water
	flour for dusting

- Blanch the saffron in 3–4 tablespoons of hot water. When deep yellow, add the strained liquid to the flour mixture instead of the hot water for home-made egg noodles.

Home-made Green Noodles

NOUILLES VERTES

SERVES 4

200g (7oz)	strong plain white flour, sieved
25g (1oz)	fine semolina
½ tablespoon	olive oil
1	egg
	a pinch of salt
50g (2oz)	spinach purée, squeezed dry
	a little warm water
	flour for dusting

- Add the spinach purée, with a little warm water if necessary, to the flour mixture instead of the hot water in the recipe for home-made egg noodles.

Home-made Black Noodles

NOUILLES À L'ENCRE

SERVES 4

200g (*7oz*)	strong plain white flour, sieved
25g (*1oz*)	fine semolina
½ tablespoon	olive oil
1	egg
	a pinch of salt
2–3 tablespoons	reduced squid ink, plus a little warm water if necessary
	flour for dusting

- Buy very fresh squid with unbroken ink sacs, so that as much ink as possible can be collected. About 1kg (*2¼lb*) squid should provide enough ink to reduce, by simmering, to the required quantity of 2–3 tablespoons. If necessary, make the amount up with a little warm water.

- Add ink, or ink and water, to the flour mixture instead of the hot water in the recipe for home-made egg noodles, along with the egg.

SOUPS
AND
STEWS

Cod Ragout with Saffron

RAGOÛT DE CABILLAUD AU SAFRAN

SERVES 4

720g (1½–1¾lb)	fillet of cod, bones carefully removed
1	small shallot, finely chopped
20g (¾oz)	butter
100ml (4fl oz)	dry white wine
200ml (7fl oz)	fish stock (see page 22)
250ml (8fl oz)	double cream
	a few strands of saffron
80g (3oz)	tomatoes, blanched, skinned, deseeded and diced
	salt, cayenne pepper

- Cut the cod into neat strips each weighing about 15g (½oz), and season with salt and cayenne pepper.

- Sweat the shallot in the butter for 2–3 minutes until transparent, and then add the cod. Add the white wine and the fish stock, and poach the fish for 1 minute.

- Take out the cod and keep warm. Reduce the stock by half by boiling fast and then add the cream and the saffron. Boil for 2–3 minutes.

- Stir in the tomatoes, season with salt and cayenne and finally drop in the pieces of fish.

- Divide between four suitable plates and serve immediately.

Prawn and Bream Curry

SERVES 4

450g (*1lb*)	fillet of bream, skinned, carefully boned and cut into dice
225g (*8oz*)	raw prawns, peeled
	the juice of half a lemon
	flour to dust the fish
1 tablespoon	vegetable oil
1	medium onion, finely chopped
½ teaspoon	each of ground fenugreek, turmeric and cumin
1	medium cooking apple, peeled and finely chopped
250ml (*8fl oz*)	fish stock (see page 22)
25g (*1oz*)	raisins
250ml (*8fl oz*)	double cream
250g (*8½oz*)	tomatoes, blanched, skinned, deseeded and diced
½ teaspoon	garam masala
	salt and cayenne pepper
	almond flakes, lightly toasted, to garnish

- Sprinkle the lemon juice over the bream dice, then season with salt and cayenne pepper and dust with flour. Leave to rest for about 10 minutes.

- Heat the oil in a heavy frying pan and lightly sauté the dusted fish for about 2 minutes until golden brown. Remove and keep warm.

- Add the onion and sweat with the fenugreek, turmeric and cumin until soft. Stir in the apple and sauté further until soft. Pour on the fish stock and reduce by half.

- Add the raisins, cream and tomatoes. Reduce for 3–4 minutes, then gently stir in the fish and seasoned prawns and bring the contents of the pan to the boil.

- Carefully season with garam masala, salt and cayenne and serve immediately, garnished with almond flakes.

Note Serve the curry with basmati rice flavoured with green cardamom pods.
The brilliant yellow of turmeric may stain a wooden worktop or a wooden spoon because of the porous nature of wood; it is a good idea to keep a special spoon reserved for stirring curries.

Chilled Consommé with Two Caviars

CONSOMMÉ FROID AUX DEUX CAVIARS

SERVES 4

200g (*7oz*)	white fish fillet (such as whiting, cod or pike), skinned, carefully boned and finely chopped
50g (*2oz*)	parsnips, peeled ⎫
50g (*2oz*)	leeks ⎬ chopped
50g (*2oz*)	shallots ⎭
1	sprig of thyme
½	bay leaf
1	sprig of parsley
1	egg white, lightly beaten
1.2 litres (*2 pints*)	cold fish stock (see page 22)
50g (*2oz*)	Beluga or Sevruga caviar
20g (*¾oz*)	salmon caviar
	salt, freshly ground pepper
	snipped chives to garnish

- Mix the vegetables with the finely chopped raw fish. Add the herbs and egg whites.

- Pour the cold fish stock over the mixture and leave to rest for half an hour, stirring occasionally. Then in a large pan bring it slowly to the boil, stirring almost continuously to prevent sticking and burning on the bottom of the pan.

- Reduce the heat as soon as the boiling starts and simmer for 15–20 minutes.

- Strain carefully and slowly through a muslin. Adjust seasoning, and cool the stock until it just starts to become jellied.

- Divide between four soup plates and arrange the caviar as shown in the photograph. Garnish with chives and serve immediately.

Eel Soup

SOUPE D'ANGUILLE

SERVES 4

800g (1¾lb)	eel, skinned, gutted and trimmed
100ml (4fl oz)	white wine vinegar
2	small shallots, finely chopped
1	clove of garlic, crushed
2–3	sprigs of parsley
50g (2oz)	carrots, celeriac and leek, cut into dice
700ml (1¼ pints)	fish stock (see page 22)
2	egg yolks ⎫ whisked together and strained
100ml (4fl oz)	double cream ⎭
2 tablespoons	mixed fresh herbs (thyme, sage, marjoram), finely chopped
	salt, a few crushed white peppercorns

- Cut the eel into bite-sized pieces and arrange in a deep buttered dish.

- Put the vinegar into a large pan with 600ml (1 pint) water. Add the shallots, garlic, parsley, salt and peppercorns. Bring to the boil and simmer for 10 minutes. Then pour the hot liquid over the eel pieces and set aside.

- Put the vegetables into the fish stock in a heavy pan and bring to the boil. Simmer for about 5 minutes.

- Drain the fish pieces and add them to the stock and vegetable pan. Simmer for a further 5 minutes and remove from the heat.

- Gradually add the egg-and-cream mixture to the soup, stirring constantly with a wooden spoon. Bring the soup just to the boil again, taking care that the mixture does not overheat and curdle.

- Check the seasoning and add the fresh herbs. Serve at once.

Note In this recipe the eel may be replaced by monkfish.

Fish Soup
with Slices of Sea Bass

CONSOMMÉ DE POISSON AU FILET DE LOUP DE MER

SERVES 4

120g (4½oz)	fillet of sea bass, skinned, carefully boned, and cut into fine slices	
1 litre (1¾ pints)	fish stock (see page 22), chilled	
1	egg white	
100g (4oz)	white fish (such as whiting), skinned, boned and very finely chopped	
50g (2oz)	leek, diced	to clarify the stock
1	clove of garlic, crushed	
1	medium tomato, diced	
1	sprig of tarragon	
60g (2oz)	beetroot	peeled and thinly sliced
60g (2oz)	carrots	
	salt, freshly ground pepper	
	a sprig of coriander to garnish	

- First clarify the stock: lightly beat the egg white in a pan, and add the white fish. Mix in the leek, garlic, tomato and tarragon, add the cold fish stock and bring to the boil, stirring slowly all the time. Remove from the heat and allow to stand for one hour. Strain slowly and carefully through a muslin and season.

- Meanwhile, with a cutter cut the beetroot and carrot into fish shapes and blanch in boiling, salted water for about 2 minutes.

- Make four roses from the slices of bass, season lightly with salt and arrange in the middle of individual soup plates. Add the hot strained soup and the vegetable fish, and garnish with coriander leaves.

Note Clarification causes loss of flavour, so the fish stock should ideally have a good strong flavour.

Crab Bisque

SERVES 10

2 × 500g (*1lb 2oz*)	crabs (preferably live, but cooked will do), thoroughly washed
4 tablespoons	olive oil
3 tablespoons	brandy
2	small shallots, finely chopped
25g (*1 oz*)	butter
100g (*4oz*)	leeks
100g (*4oz*)	carrots, peeled } cut into fine dice
100g (*4oz*)	celeriac, peeled
1	small clove of garlic, crushed
2	medium tomatoes, cut in half, deseeded and diced
200ml (*7fl oz*)	dry white wine
1 litre (*1¾ pints*)	fish stock (see page 22)
300ml (*½ pint*)	double cream
1 tablespoon	tarragon, snipped
100ml (*4fl oz*)	whipped cream
	salt, freshly ground pepper

- If the crabs are live, blanch them for 2 minutes in boiling water to kill them. Without removing the shell, cut the crab into small pieces and season with salt and pepper.

- In a heavy frying pan, heat the olive oil and sauté the crab for about 5 minutes until red. Add the brandy and set alight. Lower the heat and simmer for 1 minute. Remove the crab pieces.

- In the same pan, sweat the shallots in the butter for about 3 minutes, until transparent, and then add the leeks, carrots, celeriac and garlic. Sauté for 2–3 minutes more.

- Add the tomatoes, the white wine and the fish stock, and simmer for 5 minutes.

- Remove the crab from the shell and set the meat aside (you can use the shells for crab butter or stock).

- Allow the soup to simmer gently for a further 20–30 minutes. If necessary add more fish stock.

- Add the double cream and the tarragon and allow to simmer for another 5 minutes.

- Strain the crab bisque through a fine sieve or muslin and bring to boiling point. Remove from the heat, carefully fold in the whipped cream and season with salt and pepper.

- Arrange the crab meat in suitable warmed plates and add the crab bisque. Serve at once.

Crawfish Curry Soup

SERVES 4

220g (*8oz*)	crawfish flesh, diced
25g (*1oz*)	vegetable oil or clarified butter
50g (*2oz*)	shallots, finely chopped
50g (*2oz*)	celery, finely sliced
½ teaspoon	each of ground fenugreek, cumin and turmeric
1 litre (*1¾ pints*)	fish stock (see page 22)
½	bay leaf
½	clove of garlic, finely chopped
150g (*5½oz*)	tomatoes, blanched, skinned, deseeded and diced
4	sprigs of coriander leaves, finely cut
	salt and cayenne pepper

- Heat the oil or butter in a heavy pan and sweat the shallots and celery until transparent. Stir in the fenugreek, cumin and turmeric.

- Add the stock, bay leaf and garlic. Bring to the boil and simmer until reduced by one third.

- Add the crawfish and heat through for about 2 minutes.

- At the last minute, gently stir in the tomato dice and coriander leaves. Season with salt and cayenne pepper and serve in individual bowls.

Note This soup may be served with a garnish of yoghurt and dill.

Scallop Soup with Vegetables

SOUPE DE COQUILLES ST JACQUES

SERVES 4

8	large scallops in their shells (about 240g (*8oz*) net weight)
20g (*¾oz*)	carrot, peeled ⎫
30g (*1oz*)	leek ⎬ cut into fine strips
30g (*1oz*)	celery ⎭
20g (*¾oz*)	butter
200ml (*7fl oz*)	mussel stock (see page 22)
200ml (*7fl oz*)	fish stock (see page 22)
1 tablespoon	Noilly Prat
	salt, freshly ground pepper
1 tablespoon	chives, finely cut, to garnish

- Open the scallops with the tip of a strong knife and place on a warm hotplate or in a warm pan for a few minutes to open them completely.

- Remove the scallops and corals with a soup spoon. Carefully separate the scallops from the corals and wash both thoroughly to remove grit. Pat dry with kitchen towel and season with salt and pepper.

- Sweat the vegetables well in the butter without colouring, add the mussel stock and the fish stock and allow to simmer for 2–3 minutes.

- Add the scallops and corals and simmer very gently for a further 15 seconds. Stir in the Noilly Prat and season to taste.

- Divide between four warmed soup plates, garnish with the cut chives and serve immediately.

Note It is important that the scallops are poached gently to prevent them from drying out.

Lobster Chowder with Cream

There are three basic types of chowder made in New England, distinguished according to the liquid used in the cooking: milk chowder or milk-and-cream chowder, stock chowder (as used in Fisherman's Clam Chowder), or stock-and-cream chowder as in this recipe.

SERVES 4

1	live lobster, weighing about 450g (*1lb*), or 100g (*4oz*) freshly picked tail and claw meat
40g (*1½ oz*)	butter
3 tablespoons	brandy
1	small clove of garlic, finely chopped
450g (*1lb*)	very ripe tomatoes, blanched, skinned, deseeded and diced
250ml (*8fl oz*)	fish stock (see page 22)
	a pinch of ground coriander
200g (*7oz*)	baby sweetcorn
200ml (*7fl oz*)	double cream
1 tablespoon	tarragon, snipped
	salt, freshly ground pepper

- Splash the lobsters with cold water, heat a very large pan of water and when boiling drop them in; leave for 1 minute to kill them. Remove them and plunge into iced water.

- Cut the bodies in half and discard the stomachs. Remove the tails and cut each into 3 sections crosswise. Then cut the claws in half and crack with the heel of a knife. Remove the legs from the bodies.

- Heat 30g (*1oz*) of the butter in a large pan and sauté the lobster pieces briskly for 3–4 minutes. Add the brandy, set alight, cover and reduce the heat. Simmer for 1 minute. Lift out the lobster pieces, cool, and remove the flesh. Cut into small cubes.

- In the same pan, sauté the garlic and tomatoes in the remaining butter for 1 minute. Deglaze with a little stock.

- Add the lobster meat, coriander, sweetcorn, cream, and the rest of the stock.

- Simmer gently for long enough to let the flavours blend. Add the snipped tarragon leaves, season to taste and serve immediately.

Fisherman's Clam Chowder

SERVES 4

24	cherrystone clams, scrubbed and cleaned
750ml (*27fl oz*)	fish stock (see page 22)
25g (*1oz*)	onion ⎤
25g (*1oz*)	leek ⎟
25g (*1oz*)	carrot, peeled ⎬ cut into small dice
50g (*2oz*)	celeriac, peeled ⎦
1	clove of garlic, crushed
20g (*¾oz*)	butter
1	small bay leaf
25g (*1oz*)	green pepper, deseeded and cut into small dice
100g (*4oz*)	potato, peeled and cut into small dice
2	tomatoes, blanched, skinned, deseeded and diced
1 teaspoon	fresh thyme ⎤ chopped
1 teaspoon	parsley ⎦
	salt, freshly ground pepper

- Place the clams in a large pan with the stock. Cover and simmer until the clams open. Remove them from the stock and leave to cool. Strain the stock through a muslin or a fine sieve and reserve.

- Take the clams out of the shells and cut away the hard white tendons. Dice the flesh.

- Sauté the onion, leek, carrot, celeriac and garlic in the butter, without browning. Add the bay leaf, green pepper, potato and reserved stock, and simmer for about 7–8 minutes.

- Add the tomatoes and simmer for a further minute. Remove the bay leaf, then stir in the clams and the herbs. Season to taste with salt and pepper.

Note This dish is also very good served cold.

Oyster Soup with Champagne

POTAGE AUX HUÎTRES ET AU CHAMPAGNE

SERVES 4

16	oysters, Colchester or Belon
1	small shallot, finely chopped
10g (½oz)	butter
200ml (7fl oz)	fish stock (see page 22)
150ml (¼ pint)	champagne
100ml (4fl oz)	whipped cream ⎫ mixed together
1	egg yolk ⎭
	salt, freshly ground pepper
1 tablespoon	dill, cut, to garnish

- Open the oysters with a small, strong knife, and remove them from their shells; cut away the hard tendons (strain and keep any oyster liquor).

- In a saucepan, sauté the shallot in the butter until transparent. Add the fish stock, oyster juice and champagne, and reduce by half.

- Drop the oysters into the pan and remove almost immediately; keep warm.

- Stir the cream-and-egg mixture into the stock. Heat gently but do not boil. Liquidise or work with a hand blender until light and frothy.

- Add the oysters and season to taste with salt and pepper. Arrange four oysters in each of four warmed soup plates and divide the hot soup between them. Garnish with dill and serve immediately.

Fish Pot-au-Feu

POT-AU-FEU DE POISSON

The vegetables may be altered according to the season, but be sure you always use red peppers or tomatoes as it is their red colour that is typical of this dish.

SERVES 4

600g (*1lb 5oz*)	seafish fillets (eg turbot, red mullet, bass), boned (skin the turbot and keep the skin, and the bones and heads of all the fish)
8	mussels, soaked, scrubbed and beard removed
25g (*1oz*)	butter
1	large onion, chopped
½	stick of celery
2–3	sprigs of parsley
1	clove of garlic, finely chopped
1	small piece of red chilli, finely chopped
	a few strands of saffron
4	small carrots, peeled ⎫
2	small leeks ⎬ cut into large strips
1	courgette ⎭
1	red pepper, deseeded and cut into fine strips
4	small slices of white bread
	salt, freshly ground pepper

- Cut the fish fillets into pieces of equal size and season with salt and pepper. Set aside.

- Heat the butter in a deep pan, add the onion and sweat quickly until transparent.

- Add the fish heads and bones and the turbot skin, the celery, parsley, garlic and chilli, then 1 litre (*1¾ pints*) of water, and a little salt and pepper. Bring to the boil and simmer for 10 minutes. Strain through a muslin or a fine sieve into a clean pan.

- Season the liquid with the saffron and a little salt and pepper.

- Add the rest of the vegetables and simmer until just done. Remove the vegetables with a skimming ladle and keep warm.

- Arrange the mussels in a steaming basket.

- Bring the pan of stock to a simmer, cover the mussels and steam over the stock for about 3 minutes until the shells open. Remove and keep warm (discarding any that do not open).

- Add the pieces of fish to the steaming basket, skin side facing down, and steam for 1 minute.

- Meanwhile, toast the slices of bread.

- Arrange the fish, mussels with top shells removed and vegetables on warmed plates, and cover with the well seasoned bouillon.

- Serve toast separately.

Fish Soup with Mussels

SOUPE DE POISSON AUX MOULES

Fennel herb is widely available now, but if you can't find it, use some finely sliced bulb or the feathery leaves of the bulb instead. Its flavour is enhanced in this soup by the Pernod.

SERVES 4

300g (*11oz*)	monkfish tail, skinned, bone removed and cut into small pieces
500g (*1lb 2oz*)	mussels, soaked and scrubbed and beards removed
1 litre (*1¾ pints*)	fish stock (see page 22)
2	small shallots, finely chopped
45g (*1¾oz*)	butter
200g (*7oz*)	celery, cut into small pieces
1	fennel bulb, cut into small pieces
1	large tomato, blanched, skinned, deseeded and diced
1	bay leaf
100g (*4oz*)	white bread, cut into pieces 1cm (*½in*) thick
1 tablespoon	Pernod
	a little fennel herb, finely chopped
	salt, freshly ground pepper

- In a large saucepan, heat the fish stock. Drop in the mussels and simmer for 3–4 minutes until the mussels have opened (discard any that stay closed). Remove the mussels from their shells and set aside.

- Sweat the shallots in a third of the butter until transparent, add the celery and fennel, tomato and bay leaf and sweat for 2–3 minutes more.

- Strain the mussel cooking stock carefully to remove any grit and add to the vegetables. Cover and simmer for 6–7 minutes. Season with salt and pepper.

- Add the fish to the soup and simmer uncovered for about 2 minutes.

- Meanwhile, sauté the bread on both sides in the remaining butter until golden.

- Stir the Pernod, mussels and fennel herb into the soup, and check seasoning. Serve in a tureen or in individual warmed soup plates, with the bread at the side.

Bouillabaisse

You can substitute any similar fish and shellfish, according to what is in season.

SERVES 4

150g (5½oz)	fillet of sea bass	⎫
150g (5½oz)	fillet of scorpion fish	⎬ with skin, scaled and carefully boned
150g (5½oz)	fillet of red mullet	⎭
150g (5½oz)	monkfish tail, skinned	
4	scampi in their shells	
2	small squid, each weighing about 50g (2oz)	
4	mussels, soaked, scrubbed thoroughly, beards removed	
8	scallops in their shells	
	the juice of half a lemon	
100g (4oz)	onion, finely chopped	
50g (2oz)	leek, white part only	⎫
100g (4oz)	fennel	⎬ cut into strips
50g (2oz)	carrots, peeled	⎭
50ml (2fl oz)	olive oil	
2	cloves of garlic, crushed	
	a few strands of saffron	
4	medium tomatoes, blanched, peeled, deseeded and diced	
200ml (7fl oz)	dry white wine	
400ml (14fl oz)	fish stock (see page 22)	
1 tablespoon	Pernod	
1 tablespoon	fennel herb, finely cut	
	salt, finely ground pepper	

For the mussels

1	small shallot, finely chopped
100ml (4fl oz)	dry white wine
	a few sprigs of parsley

- Cut the fish fillets into pieces and, keeping the different fish separate, marinate with salt, pepper and lemon juice until needed.

- Shell the scampi, leaving on the tail sections, and marinate in the same way.

- Holding the squid by the tentacles, pull off the heads; remove the insides and quills. Cut off the tentacles and cut the squid into rings. Marinate as for the fish and scampi.

- Put the mussels, with their shallot, wine and parsley, in a covered pan, bring to the boil, and allow to simmer for about 3–4 minutes. Discard any mussels that have not opened and set them aside in their shells in a warm place. Strain the liquid through a muslin into a clean pan and reduce by half by fast boiling. Reserve.

- Meanwhile, open the scallops with a strong, small knife and put them in a pan or on a hotplate to open completely. Remove the scallops and roe with a soup spoon, separate and wash thoroughly. Season and set aside.

- In a wide casserole, sweat the onion, leek, fennel and carrots in the olive oil for 4–5 minutes, stirring constantly.

- Add the garlic, saffron and tomatoes and sauté for 3–5 minutes.

- Add the white wine, the fish stock and the reduced mussel stock, and then gently drop in the monkfish, the squid and the scorpion fish; let them poach for 1 minute, then add the rest of the fish, the scampi and the scallops and roe.

- Season with the Pernod and salt and pepper to taste, and the fennel herb.

- Arrange the soup, fish and shellfish, and the mussels, in four warmed soup plates and serve immediately.

Note Freshly toasted French bread spread with garlic butter gives this dish a special note. Small fish may be served whole, but pieces of filleted fish are easier for your guests to manage.

Seafood in Basil Sauce

RENDEZVOUS DE FRUITS DE MER À LA CRÈME DE BASILIC

This *rendezvous* may be made with whatever fish or shellfish is available or in season.

SERVES 4

4	large scallops in their shells, net weight about 120g (4½oz)
4	oysters
8	scampi, shelled and washed
140g (5oz)	each of salmon and turbot fillet, cut lengthways into 15-g (½-oz) pieces
20g (¾oz)	carrot, leek, celery, peeled and trimmed and cut into thin strips
20g (¾oz)	butter
3 scant tablespoons	Noilly Prat
100ml (4fl oz)	dry white wine
200ml (7fl oz)	fish stock (see page 22)
250ml (8fl oz)	double cream
12	basil leaves
50ml (2fl oz)	champagne
	salt, freshly ground pepper

- Open the scallops with the tip of a strong knife. Remove the scallops and corals and wash thoroughly and quickly to remove all the grit. Cut in half into two discs and dry.

- Open the oysters, remove from their shells and cut away the tendon. Strain the oyster liquor carefully, place the rinsed oysters in it, and set aside.

- Sweat the vegetables in the butter, add the Noilly Prat and white wine and bring to the boil.

- Add the fish stock and boil to reduce by two-thirds. Then add the cream and boil gently to reduce to the required consistency.

- Season the fish and shellfish pieces and add to the sauce. Simmer for about 2 minutes.

- Cut the basil leaves into fine strips and add to the sauce with a dash of champagne. Season to taste and serve immediately.

Mixed Fish Soup with Vegetables

POT-AU-FEU DE POISSON

SERVES 4

120g (4¹⁄₂oz)	fillet of sea bass	
80g (3oz)	fillet of Scottish salmon	} with skin, carefully boned
80g (3oz)	fillet of red mullet	
80g (3oz)	fillet of turbot	
60g (2oz)	fillet of sole	} skinned and carefully boned
400ml (14fl oz)	fish consommé (see page 40), flavoured with a few strands of saffron	
12	baby carrots with stalks, scraped	
12	cherry tomatoes, blanched and peeled	
8	baby parsnips with stalks, scraped	
	salt, freshly ground pepper	

- Cut the fish pieces into small cubes. Season with salt and pepper.

- Gently heat the consommé.

- Meanwhile, steam the vegetables until just tender, and season. Keep warm. Steam the fish pieces over the hot consommé for 30 seconds.

- Arrange the fish and vegetables in four warmed soup plates and then ladle in the hot consommé. Serve immediately.

FIRST COURSES

Crab Salad with Coconut

SALADE DE CRABE À MA FAÇON

SERVES 4

225g (*8oz*)	white crab meat
1	small shallot, finely chopped
1	tomato, blanched, skinned, deseeded and cut into thin strips
1	stick of celery, trimmed and cut into thin strips
50g (*2oz*)	fine green beans, trimmed, blanched and cut into strips
25g (*1oz*)	fresh coconut, shredded
	the juice of half a lemon
1	grafefruit } peeled, pith removed and segmented
1	orange } (reserve juice)
	salt, freshly ground pepper
	chervil sprigs to garnish

- Mix together the crab meat, shallot, tomato and celery strips, green beans and coconut. Moisten with the lemon, orange and grapefruit juices and season to taste with salt and pepper.

- Arrange the fruit segments on four plates, spoon the crab mixture on top and garnish with chervil sprigs. Serve well chilled.

Lobster Salad with Asparagus, Port Wine Mayonnaise Sauce

SALADE DE HOMARD ET ASPERGES AU PORTO

SERVES 4

1	live lobster, weighing 600–800g (1¼–1¾lb)
20	spears young, thin, green asparagus
	a few sprigs of tarragon, finely snipped
	salt, freshly ground pepper

Port wine mayonnaise sauce

100ml (*4fl oz*)	red wine
100ml (*4fl oz*)	red port
1	small shallot, finely chopped
1	egg yolk
100ml (*4fl oz*)	groundnut oil
	salt, freshly ground pepper

Salad

a few leaves each of
  frisée lettuce ⎤
  radicchio ⎥ washed and
  watercress ⎰ carefully dried
  oak-leaf lettuce ⎦

Dressing

1 tablespoon	red wine vinegar ⎤	mixed together
4 tablespoons	walnut oil ⎰	and seasoned

- Splash the lobster with cold water, then plunge it into boiling water. Remove the pan from the heat but leave the lobster in the liquid for 10 minutes; take out the lobster and leave to cool (save a little of the liquid for the sauce).

- Cut the asparagus about 7cm (*3in*) from the head and boil the spears in salted water until *al dente*. Remove and plunge them into iced water. Drain and set aside.

- *To make the port wine mayonnaise:* bring to the boil the red wine and port with the shallot. Reduce until a tablespoon remains. Leave to cool.
  Whisk the egg yolk with the cooled mixture until it is light and thick.
  Gradually beat in the oil, a few drops at a time to begin with. Season to taste. You may need to thin the mixture down with a drop of wine or warm lobster cooking liquid.

- Remove the lobster meat from the shells, discarding the intestines. Cut the tail into medallions and the claws in half. Season lightly with salt and pepper.

- Sprinkle the lobster with tarragon and coat lightly with some of the prepared dressing. Toss the asparagus spears and salad leaves in the rest of the dressing.

- To serve, place a spoonful of the mayonnaise sauce on to each of four cold plates. Arrange the salad leaves, asparagus and lobster as desired on each plate.

A Composition of Salads with Gilt-head Bream and White Butter Sauce

Any salad leaves can be used for this recipe, depending on the season. You can also substitute whatever fish is available.

SERVES 4

4	fillets of gilt-head bream, each weighing about 100g (*4oz*)
	the juice of half a lemon
1 tablespoon	olive oil
1	small radicchio lettuce heart ⎫
1	small curly lettuce heart ⎬ washed and dried
1	small oak-leaf lettuce heart ⎭
	half a bunch of watercress
4	cherry tomatoes
	salt, freshly ground pepper

Vinaigrette

90ml (*3fl oz*)	olive oil
2 tablespoons	white wine vinegar
	salt, freshly ground pepper

White butter sauce

100ml (*4fl oz*)	dry white wine
1	small shallot, finely chopped
80g (*3oz*)	butter, chilled and cut into cubes
	salt, freshly ground pepper

- *To make the sauce:* put the wine in a pan with the shallot and boil rapidly to reduce by half. Remove from the heat and gradually whisk in the butter cubes. Season with salt and pepper and keep warm.

- Season the fish fillets with salt, pepper and lemon juice. Sauté in hot olive oil for 1 minute on each side, without browning.

- Meanwhile, tear the salad leaves into neat pieces, mix together the vinaigrette ingredients and then dress the leaves. Arrange on four plates.

- Place the fillets on the dressed salads, and serve immediately with a little butter sauce spooned over. Garnish with a cherry tomato.

Fish Terrine with White Asparagus

TERRINE DE POISSON AUX ASPERGES BLANCHES

SERVES 10

300g (*11oz*)	fillet of pike, skinned and carefully boned
400g (*14oz*)	thin white asparagus, peeled and blanched
250ml (*8fl oz*)	double cream
50ml (*2fl oz*)	Noilly Prat
20g (*¾oz*)	lobster eggs
15g (*½oz*)	black truffles, chopped (optional)
2 tablespoons	flat-leaf parsley, finely chopped
100g (*4oz*)	fresh or 10g (*¼oz*) dried morels, soaked and cleaned
60g (*2oz*)	kipper pâté (see page 74)
	salt, freshly ground pepper
	whole chives to garnish

- Cut the pike fillet into pieces and season with salt and pepper. Chill it and the cream in the freezer for 10 minutes.

- In a chilled food processor, blend the fish with the cream and Noilly Prat until smooth.

- Pass through a tamis sieve and gently fold in the lobster eggs, truffles and parsley. Check seasoning.

- Preheat the oven to 150°C/300°F/Gas 2.

- Remove the stalks from the morels, and stuff them with the kipper pâté.

- Rub a 1.5-litre (*2½-pint*) terrine well with butter. Lay two-thirds of the asparagus on the bottom and along the long sides. Spoon half the fish mousse into the terrine, and arrange a row of morels along the middle of the terrine, from one end to the other. Cover them with the rest of the mousse and finish with the rest of the asparagus.

- Poach, covered, in a bain-marie in the oven for 35–40 minutes.

- Remove from the oven and cool completely and then place a light weight on top to ensure that the texture is as firm as possible.

- To serve, arrange a slice of terrine on individual cold plates and garnish with chives.

Note The terrine can be served with a cold herb sauce (see page 28).

Fish Terrine with Spinach

TERRINE DE POISSON AUX ÉPINARDS

SERVES 10

400g (*14oz*)	fillet of pike, skinned and carefully boned
190g (*7oz*)	fresh fish fillet, such as gilt-head bream, red mullet, bass and scallops – or whatever you prefer or is available
50ml (*2fl oz*)	olive oil
100ml (*4fl oz*)	dry white vermouth ⎫ chilled
400ml (*14fl oz*)	double cream ⎭
100g (*4oz*)	fresh or 10g (*¼oz*) dried morels, soaked, washed and chopped
250g (*8½oz*)	spinach leaves, thick stalks removed, blanched and well drained
	freshly ground nutmeg
	salt, freshly ground pepper

- Cut the pike into biggish pieces, season and chill.

- Trim the fresh fish fillets and cut them into bite-sized pieces. Season with salt and pepper, pour on the olive oil and chill.

- In a chilled food processor, blend the pike with a couple of ice cubes until smooth. Add the very cold vermouth, half the cream, a grating of nutmeg and some salt and pepper. Purée again well.

- Pass this mixture through a tamis sieve into a bowl and place the bowl in a basin of ice to keep the mixture cool. Gently fold in the rest of the cream. Chill.

- Preheat the oven to 140°C/275°F/Gas 1. Lightly oil a 1.5-litre (*2½-pint*) terrine with a lid. Line it with cling film, leaving enough at the top to cover the dish and then rinse it out with water.

- Mix the chopped morels with one tenth of the pike mousseline. Drain the fish pieces of any liquid and add to the morel mixture.

- Lay out the spinach leaves side by side on a cloth, overlapping them; the spinach 'blanket' should be the same length as the terrine. Place the fish-and-morel mixture along the middle, fold over the spinach leaves and roll into a sausage about 3cm (*1in*) thick.

- Spoon half of the mousseline mixture carefully into the terrine, tapping the terrine to make sure there are no air bubbles. Place the spinach sausage in the middle and cover with the rest of the mousseline.

- Fold over the cling film, cover the terrine with a lid and poach in a bain-marie in the oven for about 50 minutes.

- If you are serving the terrine hot allow it to cool slightly before turning it out; or leave it to cool completely before turning it out if you are serving it cold.

Note This dish is delicious served as a cold starter with Sauce Moscovite (see page 26) or Herb Sauce (see page 28), or served warm with salad.

Potted Crab and Asparagus

SERVES 4

300g (*11oz*)	white crab meat
	the juice of 1 lime
2 teaspoons	brandy
	a pinch of paprika
100g (*4oz*)	butter, softened
50g (*2oz*)	mayonnaise
25g (*1oz*)	salmon caviar
	salt and cayenne pepper
8	asparagus tips
	the zest of half a lime } blanched, to garnish

- Place the crab in a dish and season with the lime juice and some salt.

- Warm the brandy in a small saucepan and add a little paprika.

- Mix the butter and the mayonnaise in a bowl; then strain on the brandy and paprika. Gently stir in the crab meat, mix well to bind together and season lightly with cayenne pepper. Finally, stir in the salmon caviar.

- Divide the mixture between four individual ramekin dishes and leave to rest at room temperature for 10 minutes or so.

- To serve, garnish each dish with 2 asparagus tips and a little lime zest.

Smoked Haddock Mousse

MOUSSE D'AIGLEFIN FUMÉ

SERVES 4

400g (*14oz*)	fillet of smoked haddock, skinned and carefully boned
50g (*2oz*)	carrot, peeled
50g (*2oz*)	onion — sliced
50g (*2oz*)	celery
1	bay leaf
	a few sprigs of parsley
	a few white peppercorns
3	leaves of gelatine, softened in cold water and squeezed dry
	the juice of half a lemon
250ml (*8fl oz*)	double cream
1 tablespoon	red lumpfish roe
	salt, cayenne, freshly ground pepper
2	tablespoons soured cream
	a few thin French beans, blanched
	a few broad beans, blanched and skinned — to garnish
	chervil leaves

- Put 500ml (*16fl oz*) water into a large pan, add the carrot, onion, celery, herbs and peppercorns, and bring to the boil. Simmer for 10 minutes.

- Add the haddock fillet and poach gently for about 7 minutes. Remove the fish and flake it.

- Meanwhile, continue to boil the cooking liquid for a few minutes more, or until it has reduced to 125ml (*¼ pint*). Add the softened gelatine and stir until it has dissolved. Strain the liquid.

- Blend the flaked fish and the cooking liquid in a food processor or a blender until smooth. Season carefully with freshly ground pepper, a pinch of cayenne pepper and lemon juice to taste (and salt if necessary).

- Lightly whip the double cream and, keeping 2 tablespoons aside, fold into the haddock mixture. Check seasoning. Pour into individual ramekins or into one container if you are going to make quenelles (opposite) and leave to set in the refrigerator for about half an hour.

- There are various ways to serve the mousse: you can serve it in the ramekin dishes, in which case spread the remaining double cream on top of the mousse and sprinkle with lumpfish roe, or you can turn the mousses out of the dishes, in which case coat the mousses with cream and roe once turned out; you can also make quenelles (see photograph opposite) – to do this spread the cream and roe on the mousse while it is still in one large container, and then scoop out quenelle portions with a hot, wet spoon.

- Garnish with the soured cream, beans and chervil leaves.

Smoked Haddock Soufflé

SOUFFLÉ D'AIGLEFIN FUMÉ

SERVES 4

200g (7oz)	fillet of smoked haddock, skinned and carefully boned
300ml (½ pint)	milk
40g (1½oz)	butter
40g (1½oz)	plain flour
40g (1½oz)	fresh Parmesan cheese, finely grated
4	eggs, separated
	freshly ground pepper

- Cut the fish into four pieces and season it with pepper. Put it into a large pan. Add the milk and enough cold water to just cover. Bring to the boil, cover and simmer gently for about 5 minutes.

- Remove fish and strain the stock. Measure 190ml (7fl oz) and set aside to cool.

- Flake the fish and cut it finely.

- Preheat the oven to 200°C/400°F/Gas 6.

- Melt the butter in a pan, add the flour to make a roux and cook for 1 minute, stirring. Add the reserved cold fish stock and blend in well. Bring to the boil and simmer for a further 3 minutes.

- Add the fish and the cheese to the sauce, mix well and remove from the heat. Cool the mixture a little and stir in the egg yolks, one at a time. Cool the mixture a little more and check the seasoning.

- Whisk the egg whites until stiff and carefully fold them into the mixture.

- Spoon into four buttered ramekin dishes and bake in the oven for about 10–12 minutes or until risen and just set.

Note If you prefer, you can make the soufflé in one large dish, in which case bake it for about 20 minutes.

Mousse of Arbroath Smokies with Sherry and Pommery Mustard Sauce

SERVES 4

200g (7oz)	Arbroath smokies, skinned, filleted, carefully boned and flaked
3	leaves of gelatine, softened in cold water and squeezed dry
100ml (4fl oz)	fish stock (see page 22)
100ml (4fl oz)	double cream
1 teaspoon	dry sherry
	salt, cayenne pepper

Sherry and Pommery mustard sauce

1 teaspoon	sherry vinegar
2 teaspoons	Pommery mustard
125ml (5fl oz)	double cream
1 tablespoon	chives, finely cut

4	sprigs of chervil
2	tomatoes, blanched, skinned, deseeded, and cut into petals } to garnish

- *To make the mousse:* add the gelatine to the stock and warm gently until dissolved; then pour it into a blender. Add the fish and blend until smooth. Transfer to a bowl and set the bowl over a basin of ice to keep the ingredients cool. Carefully work in the cream and sherry. Season with salt and cayenne, cover the bowl with cling film, and chill the mousse for about half an hour until firm.

- *To make the sauce:* mix the sherry vinegar with the mustard; then add the cream. Stir in the chives and check the seasoning.

- To serve, pour some sauce on to each of four cold plates. With a hot, wet spoon, make quenelles with the mousse (see photograph of smoked haddock mousse, page 71) and place them on the sauce. Garnish with sprigs of chervil and tomato petals.

Kipper Pâté

Fish mousses are traditionally bound together with egg whites; in these recipes the egg whites are omitted because I have found that fish set sufficiently without them and because they tend to make the finished mousse rather dry.

SERVES 10

250g (8½oz)	white fish fillets, skinned, carefully boned and minced	
250g (8½oz)	kipper fillets, skinned, carefully boned and minced *plus*	
100g (4oz)	kipper fillets, skinned and carefully boned	chilled
2 tablespoons	Noilly Prat	
250ml (8fl oz)	double cream	
4	spinach leaves, blanched and refreshed	
20g (¾oz)	butter, softened	
	salt, freshly ground pepper	

- Preheat the oven to 150°C/300°F/Gas 2.

- Mix the minced white fish with the minced kipper in a bowl set over a basin of ice to keep the mixture cool.

- Gradually beat in the Noilly Prat and double cream and then season carefully with salt and pepper.

- Wrap the whole kipper fillets in the blanched spinach leaves.

- Grease a 1.5-litre (2½-pint) terrine with the butter. Half fill the terrine with mousse. Take the wrapped fillets, trim to fit, and place lengthwise on the mousse, in the centre of the terrine. Fill the terrine with the remaining mousse and cover with a lid or with foil.

- Poach in a bain-marie in the preheated oven for 1¼ hours. Remove from the oven and leave to go cold.

- To serve, turn out the terrine, cut into slices, and arrange slices on individual cold plates. For a special occasion, garnish with tomato roses, fine strips of blanched cucumber skin and carrot leaves on a mirror of fish aspic (see photograph).

Note The pâté can be served with mayonnaise flavoured with mustard or with a horseradish sauce.

Grilled King Prawns with Pistachio, Miso and Mustard Sauce

CREVETTES GRILLÉES AUX PISTACHES À LA MISO ET MOUTARDE

Miso is a fermented soy bean paste widely used as a seasoning in Japanese and other Eastern cuisines. There are many varieties and all are rich in nutrients and flavour. It can be bought from Oriental grocers or health food shops.

SERVES 4

8	raw king prawns
2 tablespoons	sesame oil

Miso and mustard sauce

2	egg yolks
2 tablespoons	non-sweet white miso paste
1 teaspoon	rice vinegar
1 tablespoon	dry white wine
1 teaspoon	English mustard
	a dash of light soy sauce
50g (2oz)	butter, melted and clarified
	salt, freshly ground pepper
25g (1oz)	pistachio nuts, ground or finely chopped

- Remove the shells from the prawns, leaving the last section of shell at the tail end. Devein, clean and pat dry. Cut the prawns lengthwise along the undersides and open them out to lie flat. Make an incision at the top end of each prawn, roll them up, and thread the tails through. Rub with oil, season with salt and pepper and leave to marinate until required.

- *To make the sauce:* place all the ingredients for the sauce except the butter in a double saucepan or in a basin over a pan of barely simmering water. Heat, stirring all the time, until the mixture thickens (as for a Hollandaise sauce). Take off the heat. Cool slightly and slowly incorporate the butter, whisking constantly. Strain and season the sauce. Keep warm.

- Grill the prawns under a moderate heat for 3–5 minutes, turning once.

- To serve, spoon a little of the sauce on to each of four warmed plates and place the prawns on top. Scatter with the pistachios.

Note The sauce may be adjusted according to taste with the miso and mustard.

Barbecued Hake Kebabs with Pink Grapefruit

SERVES 4

675g (1½lb)	fillets of hake, skinned, carefully boned, and rolled up neatly
3	pink grapefruit, skinned and segmented
4 teaspoons	groundnut oil
1	fennel bulb ⎫ the 'layers' separated, cut into 1.5-cm (¾-in)
1	medium onion ⎭ pieces and blanched
4	medium tomatoes, blanched, skinned, cut into quarters and deseeded

Marinade

1	clove of garlic
250ml (8fl oz)	tomato juice
	a dash of sherry
	a dash of soy sauce
	the juice of 1 lemon
	salt

Sauce

100g (4oz)	plain yoghurt
	a dash of Angostura bitters
1 tablespoon	dill ⎫ finely cut
1 tablespoon	chives ⎭
	salt, freshly ground pepper

- Mix together all the marinade ingredients and pour over the prepared fish rolls. Leave for 4 hours, occasionally turning the fish in the marinade.

- Remove the fish and pat dry with kitchen towel. Cut into 2.5-cm (1-in) pieces.

- Thread the fish securely on to skewers, alternating with grapefruit segments, and brush with groundnut oil. Thread the fennel, onion and tomato alternately on skewers and brush with groundnut oil.

- Lightly grill all the kebabs over charcoal for about 10 minutes, turning occasionally.

- Meanwhile mix all the ingredients together for the sauce. Season to taste.

- Serve the fish and grapefruit kebabs with the vegetable kebabs, and the sauce separately.

Scampi with Pernod Sauce

SCAMPI AMOUREUX

SERVES 4

400g (*14oz*)	scampi (without their shells)
30g (*1oz*)	butter
1	small shallot, finely chopped
20ml (*¾fl oz*)	Pernod
100ml (*4fl oz*)	dry white wine
100ml (*4fl oz*)	fish stock (see page 22)
150ml (*¼ pint*)	double cream
	a few tarragon leaves, snipped
	salt, freshly ground pepper

- Pat dry the scampi with kitchen towel and season with salt and pepper. Sauté for 1 minute in the butter with the finely chopped shallot. Flame with the Pernod. Pour in the white wine, cover and allow to simmer for 30 seconds.

- Remove the scampi and keep warm.

- Boil the juices until reduced by half and then add the fish stock.

- Reduce again by half, and then add the cream and tarragon leaves. Reduce to the required consistency, and season with salt and pepper. Stir in the scampi and serve immediately.

Note This scampi is delicious served with pilau rice.

Poached Oysters wrapped in Lettuce Leaves

HUÎTRES EN FEUILLES VERTES

SERVES 4

24	oysters (preferably Colchester)
24	green, medium lettuce leaves, blanched and refreshed, coarse stems removed
1 tablespoon	olive oil
1	small shallot, finely chopped
225ml (*8fl oz*)	fish stock (see page 22)
15g (*½oz*)	each of carrot, leek and celery, trimmed, peeled and cut into fine strips
	a squeeze of lemon juice
	salt, freshly ground pepper

- Open the oysters with a small, strong knife and carefully strain the juices into the fish stock. Remove the oysters from the shells (reserve the shells) and cut away the tendon. Season them with pepper.

- Wrap each oyster in a lettuce leaf. Wash the concave half of each shell and warm them.

- Gently sauté the shallot in the olive oil until transparent. Add the fish stock (with the oyster juices) and boil rapidly until reduced by half. Add the carrot, leek and celery strips and simmer for about 1 minute. Season to taste with lemon juice, salt and pepper.

- Add the oyster parcels and poach for 15 seconds.

- Place an oyster parcel in each warmed shell and spoon a little sauce and vegetables over them. Arrange six on each plate and serve immediately.

Grilled Scallops with Vegetable Ragout

COQUILLES ST JACQUES GRILLÉES AU RAGOÛT DES LÉGUMES

SERVES 4

16 scallops in their shells
    salt, freshly ground pepper

Vegetable ragout

1   small green courgette ⎱
1   small yellow courgette ⎰ seedy 'core' removed
1   small red pepper   ⎱
1   small yellow pepper   ⎬ seeds removed
1   small green pepper   ⎰
1   small aubergine
65ml (2½fl oz) olive oil
3   medium tomatoes, blanched, skinned, deseeded and diced
1   clove of garlic, crushed
4   basil leaves
    salt, freshly ground pepper

4   small sprigs of basil to garnish

- Open the scallops with the tip of a small, strong knife and then place them on a hotplate or in a warm pan to open completely. Remove the scallops carefully with a soup spoon, trim and pat dry (save the corals for another dish). Brush them with oil and season lightly. Set aside until needed.

- *To make the ragout:* cut all the vegetables into dice. Heat the olive oil in a pan and sauté the vegetables with the tomato dice and garlic for a few minutes (they should remain crisp). Season with salt and pepper. Cut the basil into fine strips, and add to the vegetable ragout. Check seasoning and allow to cool.

- Grill the scallops under a hot grill for 20 seconds each side.

- To serve, arrange the scallops on a bed of cold vegetable ragout and garnish with a sprig of basil.

Note The vegetable ragout can be served hot or cold.

Cockle Clusters
with Piquant Tomato Sauce

You can use baby clams instead of cockles in this recipe.

SERVES 4

200g (*7oz*)	cockles, cleaned
200g (*7oz*)	potatoes, peeled and cut into very fine julienne strips, and soaked in cold water for 10 minutes

Batter

1	egg yolk
100ml (*4fl oz*)	iced water
75g (*2½oz*)	plain white flour
	salt, freshly ground pepper

Sauce

1 tablespoon	olive oil
1	small onion, sliced
1	clove of garlic, sliced
500g (*1lb 2oz*)	ripe tomatoes, blanched, skinned, halved and deseeded
1	bouquet garni of onion, leek and parsley
	a pinch of sugar
	a dash of Tabasco
25g (*1oz*)	butter, chilled and cut into cubes
	salt, freshly ground pepper

vegetable oil for deep frying

- *To make the batter:* place all the ingredients in a bowl and stir. Season with salt and pepper. Do not mix it too much: the consistency should be loose. Set aside.

- *To make the sauce:* heat the oil in a saucepan and sweat the onion and garlic until transparent. Add the tomatoes, the bouquet garni and the sugar. Mix well. Moisten with a spoonful of water. Cover and simmer until soft.
  Liquidise and then strain through a sieve. Season to taste. Whisk in the butter, piece by piece, and bring back to the boil. Check seasoning and keep warm.

- Drain and pat dry the potato strips and gently mix them and the cockles with the batter so that they form a sticky mixture.

- With a large spoon, take a spoonful of this mixture and drop it into hot oil (170°C/340°F). Fry three or four at a time (but do not overcrowd the pan) until golden brown. Drain on kitchen towel.

- Meanwhile, bring the sauce back to the boil.

- Serve the clusters at once, with the sauce passed separately.

Mussels with Fennel

CASSOLETTE DE MOULES AU FENOUIL

Mussels and fennel combine to make a delicious light meal.

SERVES 4

2kg (4½lb)	mussels, soaked, scrubbed and thoroughly cleaned, beards removed
30g (1oz)	butter
2	small shallots, finely chopped
100g (4oz)	fennel bulb, cut into fine strips
200ml (7fl oz)	dry white wine
200ml (7fl oz)	fish stock (see page 22)
200ml (7fl oz)	double cream
20g (¾oz)	butter, chilled and cut into cubes
	salt, freshly ground pepper
	a few chives, cut
	a few fennel leaves, cut } to garnish

- Sweat the shallots and fennel in the butter, without browning. Add the mussels (still in their shells) white wine and stock. Cover the pan and bring to the boil. Boil only until the mussels open (3–4 minutes) or else they will become tough. Discard any that have not opened. Remove the mussels from the stock.

- Strain the stock through muslin and reduce by about half. Meanwhile, remove the mussels from their shells.

- Add the cream to the stock and reduce further until the desired consistency is achieved. Remove the pan from the heat and whisk in the butter, piece by piece. Reheat the sauce and return the mussels to it. Check the seasoning.

- Arrange in a tureen, sprinkle with the chives and fennel leaves and serve immediately.

Lemon Sole in Rice Paper

The rice paper in this recipe keeps the fish moist, making an appetising, delicate dish.

SERVES 4

4	fillets of lemon sole, each weighing about 80g (*3oz*), skinned and carefully boned
4	sheets of rice paper
4	slices of black truffle (or 4 slices of blanched and peeled red pepper)
4	long chive stems
4	sprigs of flat-leaf parsley
1 tablespoon	olive oil
1 tablespoon	clarified butter
	salt, freshly ground pepper
1	tomato, blanched, skinned, deseeded and diced } to garnish
	a little mustard and cress

- Wrap the rice paper in damp cloths until pliable.

- Season the fillets with salt and pepper. Arrange a flower on each, using a slice of truffle (or red pepper), a chive and some parsley leaves (see photograph), and then wrap each fillet in a piece of rice paper, tucking the edges neatly underneath.

- Sauté the packages gently on both sides in oil and butter until golden brown. Drain on kitchen towel.

- To serve, place a package on each of four warmed plates and garnish with the warmed and seasoned tomato, and the mustard and cress.

Fillet of Sole with Oysters

FILET DE SOLE POCHÉ AUX HUÎTRES

SERVES 4

4	fillets of sole, each weighing 60g (*2oz*)
12	fresh oysters in their shells
½ quantity	red pepper sauce (see page 28)
½ quantity	yellow pepper sauce (see page 29)
½ quantity	green pepper sauce (see page 29)
	salt, freshly ground pepper
12	sprigs of chervil to garnish

- Make the sauces as described on the above pages and keep warm.

- Season the fillets of sole with salt and pepper and steam them for 3–4 minutes.

- Carefully open the oysters with a small, strong knife and remove the top, flat shell and tendon. Steam the oysters in the bottom, concave shell for about 30 seconds, and lift the oysters out of the shells.

- Spoon a little of the three sauces on to four warmed plates, place one oyster on each sauce, garnish with chervil and arrange the sole fillets in the middle. Serve immediately.

Warm Smoked Salmon with Chives

SAUMON FUMÉ TIÈDE À LA CIBOULETTE

Smoked salmon served warm makes an unusual and delicious dish.

SERVES 4

350g (*12oz*)	Scottish smoked salmon, cut into 12 thick slices
200g (*7oz*)	small new potatoes, unpeeled
50ml (*2fl oz*)	dry white wine
100ml (*4fl oz*)	fish stock (see page 22)
1	small shallot, finely chopped
150ml (*¼ pint*)	double cream
20g (*¾oz*)	butter
300g (*11oz*)	green cabbage, cut into thin strips, blanched and well dried
2 tablespoons	whipped cream
1 tablespoon	chives, finely cut
	salt, freshly ground pepper

- Boil the potatoes in salted water until just soft. Peel and slice thinly.

- Preheat the oven to 160°C/325°F/Gas 3.

- *To make the sauce:* put the wine, stock and shallot in a pan, bring to the boil and reduce to a quarter of the original volume by rapid boiling. Add the double cream and bring back to the boil. Boil gently to reduce by half, and then strain through a fine sieve or a muslin. Season to taste with salt and pepper. Keep warm.

- Melt the butter in a saucepan and sauté the blanched cabbage for a few minutes. Season with salt and pepper and add the potato slices to warm through.

- Warm the smoked salmon in a covered oven dish in the oven for 2 minutes.

- Mix the whipped cream into the sauce and liquidise or work with a hand blender until light and frothy. Stir in the chives, check seasoning and heat through.

- To serve, arrange the cabbage and potatoes on warmed plates and carefully place the salmon on top. Spoon the sauce around the salmon and serve immediately.

Salmon and Oysters Vinaigrette

SERVES 4

200g (7oz)	fresh Scottish salmon, very thinly sliced
4	oysters (preferably Colchester), diced, liquor reserved
3 tablespoons	olive oil
1 tablespoon	white wine vinegar
1 tablespoon	chives, finely cut
	lemon juice to taste
100g (4oz)	thin asparagus, blanched
2	slices of black truffles, cut into thin strips (optional)
	salt, freshly ground pepper

- Mix together the oil and vinegar, the reserved, strained, oyster liquor and the chives. Add a little lemon juice if required and season with salt and pepper.

- Arrange the salmon on four plates, and then the diced oysters and the asparagus.

- Carefully spoon some vinaigrette over the salmon and oysters, garnish with the truffles and serve.

Note Because this fish is served raw it must be absolutely fresh.

Baked Egg with Salmon and Fennel Cream

SERVES 4

100g (4oz)	Scottish salmon, lightly poached and flaked, bones removed
100ml (4fl oz)	double cream
½	fennel bulb, finely chopped
4	eggs
4	slices of bread, for toasting
	salt, freshly ground pepper
4	sprigs of parsley to garnish

- Preheat the oven to 150°C/300°F/Gas 2.

- Heat the cream in a pan and reduce by half. Add the salmon and fennel. Season to taste.

- Butter 4 individual ramekins, and season them lightly with salt and pepper. Put an egg in each one and carefully bake in a bain-marie for 5–6 minutes or until just set.

- Spoon the cream mixture over the eggs, and serve with freshly made fingers of hot toast. Garnish with parsley.

Salmon Liver with Cabbage

FOIE DE SAUMON AU CHOU VERT

SERVES 4

200g (*7oz*)	fresh salmon liver, thinly sliced
300g (*11oz*)	green cabbage, cut into fine strips, washed and dried
40g (*1½oz*)	butter
50ml (*2fl oz*)	dry white wine
1	small shallot, finely chopped
50ml (*2fl oz*)	fish stock (see page 22)
1 tablespoon	dry sherry
	salt, freshly ground pepper and a pinch of cayenne pepper

- Heat half the butter in a pan, add the cabbage and sauté for 1 minute. Add the white wine and simmer gently, stirring occasionally. Season with salt and pepper. The cabbage must remain crisp and must not lose its colour. Drain and keep warm.

- Season the liver slices with salt and pepper and gently sauté them in the remaining butter for 15 seconds on each side. Remove and keep warm.

- Add the shallot to the frying juice, sauté for 1 minute, then add the fish stock and sherry and reduce to the required consistency. Season with salt, pepper and cayenne.

- Arrange the cabbage on warmed plates, place the liver slices on top and coat with a little sauce; serve the rest of the sauce separately.

Note Fish liver is just as delicate as calf's liver and should be handled equally carefully.

Smoked Salmon with Avocado Mousse

ROSETTE DE SAUMON FUMÉ À LA MOUSSE D'AVOCAT

SERVES 4

8	slices Scottish smoked salmon

Avocado mousse

150g (5½oz)	avocado, puréed
2	leaves of gelatine, soaked in cold water, squeezed dry and dissolved in 2 tablespoons warm water
150ml (¼ pint)	whipped cream
1 teaspoon	lemon juice
1 tablespoon	sherry
	finely grated horseradish to taste
1 teaspoon	walnut oil
	salt, freshly ground pepper

1	small avocado, cut into thin slices	
4	sprigs of chervil	} to garnish
	a little paprika	

- Take four small glass dishes or moulds and line them with the slices of smoked salmon, leaving enough salmon overlapping to fold over the top of the mousse.

- *To make the mousse:* mix the dissolved gelatine into the puréed avocado. Carefully work in the cream. Add a little lemon juice to prevent discoloration and stir in the sherry. Season with the finely grated horseradish, walnut oil and salt and pepper.

- Spoon the mousse carefully into the glass dishes and fold over the slices of salmon. Chill for about half an hour.

- Turn out on to plates and decorate with avocado slices, chervil sprigs and a dusting of paprika.

Note This dish can be prepared in advance.

Mille-Feuilles of Salmon Mousse and Caviar

MILLE-FEUILLES À LA MOUSSE DE SAUMON D'ÉCOSSE ET CAVIAR

SERVES 4

150g (5½oz)	Scottish salmon, poached, skinned, boned and chopped
1 quantity	puff pastry (see page 32)
	the juice of half a lemon
200ml (7fl oz)	whipped cream
150ml (¼ pint)	fish stock (see page 22)
1½	leaves of gelatine, softened in cold water and squeezed dry
20g (¾oz)	caviar (optional)
15g (½oz)	butter, softened
2 teaspoons	black truffle, finely chopped (optional)
20g (¾oz)	pistachio nuts, blanched, peeled and finely chopped
	flour for dusting
	salt, freshly ground pepper and a pinch of cayenne pepper
4	small slices of smoked salmon ⎱ to garnish
	a few leaves of lamb's lettuce ⎰

- Preheat the oven to 220°C/425°F/Gas 7.

- Roll out the puff pastry on a lightly floured surface to a rectangle measuring about 35 × 20cm (14 × 8in); the pastry should be 2mm (⅛in) thick. Place the pastry on a dampened baking sheet, prick it all over with a fork and bake in the hot oven until risen and crisp and golden. Leave to cool.

- Put the fish into a large basin and set over a bowl of ice to keep the mixture cool. Blend the fish with the lemon juice and season to taste. Fold in the whipped cream and check seasoning. Warm the fish stock a little and dissolve the gelatine in it. Mix carefully into the salmon mixture and then gently stir in the caviar.

- Cut the puff pastry rectangle in half; one half will be the base. Carefully spread the salmon-and-caviar mousse over the base and cover with the second half of pastry.

- Lightly brush the top with butter and sprinkle with chopped truffle and pistachio nuts. Chill in the refrigerator until set.

- Trim the edges and cut into pieces measuring about 5 × 7cm (2 × 3in). Serve one piece per person, garnished with a rose of smoked salmon and leaves of lamb's lettuce.

Raw Salmon on a Froth of Herbs

SAUMON CRU SUR UNE MOUSSE D'HERBES

This eye-catching dish needs no accompaniment other than some freshly made wholemeal toast. The green sauce can be made with many different ingredients, depending on what is available, such as watercress, burnet or balm.

SERVES 4

500g (1lb 2oz)	fillet of Scottish salmon, skinned and carefully boned
2 tablespoons	lemon juice
4 tablespoons	cold pressed olive oil
1½ teaspoons	sea salt
2 tablespoons	dill ⎫
2 tablespoons	chives ⎬ finely cut
2 tablespoons	basil ⎭
2 tablespoons	parsley ⎫ finely chopped
2 tablespoons	mustard and cress ⎬
2 tablespoons	chervil, finely snipped
	a few spinach leaves, stalks removed, finely chopped
80ml (3fl oz)	double cream
2 drops	Tabasco
	salt, freshly ground black and white pepper
	a few chervil leaves to garnish

- Cut the salmon diagonally into large, flat, thin slices and spread them out on a cold plate. Moisten the slices with 1½ tablespoons of the lemon juice and the olive oil. Season with the sea salt and set aside in a cool place.

- *To make the sauce:* put all the herbs and the spinach into a wide pan, add a tablespoon of water and heat gently for 4–5 minutes to release flavour and moisture. Strain through muslin. (You can use a juice extractor to do this if you have one.)

- Stir the cream, Tabasco, the remaining ½ tablespoon of lemon juice and seasoning into the green juice. Beat lightly with a fork or with a hand whisk until frothy. Check seasoning.

- To serve, ladle the sauce on to four cold plates. Carefully lift the salmon slices and overlap them carefully on top of the sauce. Garnish with a few torn chervil leaves.

Freshly Smoked Salmon with Cucumber, Tomato and Watercress Salad

SAUMON FRAIS FUMÉ AVEC CONCOMBRE, TOMATE ET CRESSON

Hot smoking boxes may be obtained from camping shops or in some kitchen shops; they may be purchased complete with wood dust and assembly instructions.

SERVES 4

400g (*14oz*)	fillets of Scottish salmon, skinned, carefully boned and cut into 12 equal pieces
1 tablespoon	olive oil
	salt, freshly ground pepper

Cucumber, tomato and watercress salad

100ml (*4fl oz*)	grapeseed oil
3 tablespoons	raspberry vinegar
2	ripe tomatoes, blanched, skinned, deseeded and cut into ½-cm (*¼-in*) dice
	a few sprigs of basil
¼	cucumber, peeled
1	bunch of watercress, washed, picked and dried
	salt, freshly ground pepper

Yoghurt and dill dressing

4 tablespoons	plain yoghurt
	a few sprigs of dill, finely cut
	salt, freshly ground pepper

- *To prepare the salad:* combine the oil and vinegar and sprinkle half over the tomato dice. Season and infuse with the basil.

- Cut the cucumber into strips 1 × 1 × 5cm (⅓ × ⅓ × 2in). There should be 24 strips in total. Toss the cucumber and watercress in the remaining vinaigrette. Remove, season and set aside.

- Lightly oil the salmon and season with salt and pepper. Place it in the prepared hot smoking box for about 3 minutes.

- Meanwhile, combine the yoghurt-and-dill dressing ingredients.

- To serve, place a spoonful of dill dressing in the centre of each of four cold plates. Arrange three crosses of cucumber on the dressing with a few sprigs of watercress in between each cross. Place the salmon pieces on the cucumber and spoon the tomato vinaigrette over the top. Serve immediately.

Raw Rosette of Salmon on Coriander Vinaigrette

SERVES 4

500g (*1lb 2oz*)	fillet of Scottish salmon, skinned, bones carefully removed
1½ teaspoons	sea salt
2 tablespoons	olive oil
	the juice of 1 lemon
1 teaspoon	coriander seeds, crushed
2	tomatoes, blanched, skinned, deseeded and diced
1 teaspoon	coriander leaves, finely cut *plus* 1 tablespoon leaves to garnish
	freshly ground pepper

- Cut the salmon diagonally into large, flat, thin slices, and spread them out on a cold plate. Season with the sea salt and sprinkle with half the oil and half the lemon juice. Leave to marinate for 10–15 minutes.

- Make a vinaigrette with the rest of the oil and lemon juice. Add the coriander seeds, tomato dice and cut coriander, and season with black pepper.

- To serve, arrange the salmon slices in a rosette in the middle of four cold plates. Spoon over the dressing, and decorate with fresh coriander leaves.

Marinated Salmon and Turbot

SAUMON ET TURBOT MARINÉS MARCO

SERVES 4

240g (*8½oz*)	fillet of Scottish salmon ⎱ skinned and carefully boned
200g (*7oz*)	fillet of turbot ⎰
	the juice of 1 lime
	salt
1 teaspoon	white peppercorns, crushed
1 teaspoon	coriander seeds
50ml (*2fl oz*)	olive oil
100g (*4oz*)	tomatoes, blanched, skinned, deseeded and diced
1 tablespoon	dill, finely cut

- Cut the fillets of salmon and turbot into fine strips and arrange equal amounts of each attractively on four plates.

- Sprinkle with the lime juice and season with salt, crushed peppercorns and coriander seeds. Add the olive oil, diced tomatoes and dill. Allow to stand for 3-4 minutes, then serve immediately, with warm toasted French bread if wished.

Blue Trout
with a Mousseline Sauce

TRUITE AU BLEU, SAUCE MOUSSELINE

The 'blue' of this fish comes from the bluish hue taken on by the trout's natural covering of slime when the fish is poached in vinegar; be careful when cleaning and rinsing the trout not to disturb this slimy coating. It is usual to leave the heads on trout that are to be served in this way (indeed the cheeks are considered a great delicacy).

If you wish, you can serve the trout tied into a circle, which, while not altering the taste at all, does look attractive. To do this, pull a needle and thread through the head and tail, draw them together and secure.

Use a mild vinegar, such as the herb vinegar suggested here, so that after poaching the fish there is no trace of pungent, sharp vinegar.

SERVES 4

4	river trout (or rainbow), each weighing about 200g (*7oz*), gutted
150ml (*¼ pint*)	herb vinegar
1	small onion, finely chopped
60g (*2oz*)	celeriac, cut into slices
2	sprigs of parsley, roughly chopped
6	white peppercorns, crushed
	salt
1 quantity	mousseline sauce (see page 26)
1	lemon, cut into 8 wedges ⎫ to garnish
4	sprigs of parsley ⎭

- Bring to the boil 4 litres (*7 pints*) of water with the herb vinegar, onion, celeriac, parsley, peppercorns and salt.

- Make the mousseline sauce according to the instructions on page 26. Keep warm.

- At the same time, lower the heat and poach the fish whole in the stock for 8–10 minutes.

- Carefully lift the trout out of the stock, drain and place, whole, on warmed plates. Garnish with the lemon wedges and parsley sprigs. Serve the mousseline sauce separately.

Marinated Trout Fillets with Dill Yoghurt

To make this a more elaborate dish, spoon the dill yoghurt into eight small tomato shells and top each with a teaspoonful of caviar. Serve two filled shells with each trout fillet.

SERVES 4

4	river trout, each weighing about 200g (*7oz*), cleaned, filleted, and skinned if wished (or 8 fillets, each weighing about 80g (*3oz*))
30g (*1oz*)	salt
1 tablespoon	sugar
1 tablespoon	parsley, finely chopped
4 tablespoons	dill, finely cut
	the juice of 1 lemon
300g (*11oz*)	natural yoghurt
	extra lemon juice to taste
	salt, freshly ground pepper

- Arrange the trout fillets in a single layer in a dish. Combine the salt, sugar, parsley, two-thirds of the dill and the lemon juice, and spoon over the trout. Cover and marinate in the refrigerator for 12 hours. Drain and dry the trout thoroughly.

- Combine the yoghurt and remaining cut dill. Season and add lemon juice to taste.

- Serve the fillets on a plate with the dill yoghurt at the side.

Smoked Trout with Cucumber

TRUITE FUMÉE ET FILETS DE CONCOMBRES

SERVES 4

4	fillets of smoked trout, each weighing about 50g (*2oz*), skinned and carefully boned
50g (*2oz*)	cucumber ⎤
50g (*2oz*)	radishes ⎦ cut into fine strips
50ml (*2fl oz*)	whipped cream
100g (*4oz*)	plain yoghurt
2 teaspoons	horseradish, finely grated
½ tablespoon	dill, finely cut
½	cucumber, cut with a cannelle knife and finely sliced (you will need about 40 slices)
	salt, freshly ground pepper
4	sprigs of dill ⎤
2½ tablespoons	salmon caviar ⎦ to garnish

- Cut the trout flesh into small pieces and place in a bowl. Add the cucumber strips (save a few for garnish) and the radish strips, the whipped cream, yoghurt, horseradish and cut dill, and mix together well. Season with salt and pepper.

- Position a pastry cutter in the centre of each of four plates, and fill with the trout mixture to shape into rounds. Decorate each with ten slices of cucumber and garnish attractively with salmon caviar, dill sprigs and remaining cucumber strips.

Note This dish is equally successful made with smoked salmon instead of smoked trout.

River Trout with Fresh Herbs

TRUITE DE RIVIÈRE PARFUMÉE AUX HERBES

SERVES 4

4	river trout, each weighing about 200g (*7oz*), cleaned, filleted and carefully boned (or 8 fillets, each weighing about 80g (*3oz*))
2 tablespoons	mixed herbs, finely chopped (see note)
50g (*2oz*)	butter
2 tablespoons	parsley, finely chopped
2 tablespoons	dry white wine
2 tablespoons	Madeira (medium dry)
	salt, freshly ground pepper

- Pat dry the trout, season with salt and pepper and coat generously with half the mixed herbs.

- Soften the butter in a sautéing pan with a close-fitting lid and add the trout with the rest of the mixed herbs and the parsley. Sprinkle over the wine and Madeira.

- Cover at once and allow the trout to poach gently for 2–3 minutes (poach fillets for 1½ minutes only).

- Remove the trout and place on a hot serving dish.

- Stir the cooking juices, adjust the seasoning, and pour over and around the fish. Serve at once.

Note The fresh herbs could include chives, thyme, marjoram, tarragon, dill, coriander leaves, celery leaves and basil, and perhaps a little rosemary.
You can poach the fish whole instead of filleted, if you wish, and remove the fillets when the fish is tender. It is becoming more acceptable to serve fish with skin, but this, too, is a matter of preference.

Grilled Seafood Sausage

These sausages can be served either as an hors d'oeuvre or as a main course; halve the quantity for the former, add a nice accompaniment for the latter.

Sausage skins are now easily available. The poaching will set the filling in shape, so if the skins are too firm remove them carefully before grilling.

SERVES 4

4	scallops in their shells
4	scampi, removed from their shells, about 100g (4oz) peeled weight
150g (5½oz)	fillet of Scottish salmon, skinned, boned and cut into small cubes
100g (4oz)	fillet of monkfish, skinned and cut into small cubes
150g (5½oz)	fillet of whiting or pike, skinned and boned
150ml (¼ pint)	double cream
2 teaspoons	dill, finely cut
40–50cm (16–20in)	sausage skin, soaked in water (or use cling film)
	salt, freshly ground pepper

The salmon, monkfish, whiting/pike, cream and dill are bracketed as *chilled*.

Sauce

20g (¾oz)	butter
40g (1½oz)	carrots, peeled
40g (1½oz)	leeks
40g (1½oz)	celeriac, peeled
2 tablespoons	dry white wine
100ml (4fl oz)	fish stock (see page 22)
100ml (4fl oz)	double cream
	salt, freshly ground pepper

The carrots, leeks and celeriac are bracketed as *cut into thin strips*.

- Open the scallops with a sharp knife and remove the scallops and corals with a soup spoon. Separate the scallops carefully from the corals and debris and wash quickly in cold water. Cut the scallops and corals into small dice and lay on a cloth to dry.

- Season the scallops, scampi, salmon and monkfish with salt and pepper.

- Purée the whiting or pike in a chilled food processor. Add a pinch of salt and pepper and process until smooth.

- Place the puréed fish mixture in a bowl over a basin of ice to keep cool. Gradually beat in the cream. Add all the seasoned fish and the cut dill. Season, and leave to rest for 30–40 minutes. The consistency should be like a choux paste mixture.

- Fill the sausage skin with the fish mousseline, using a piping bag or spoon, and shape into 8 sausages about 6cm (2½in) long. Bind the ends of each sausage with string.

- Poach them in hot water (do not boil) for about 5–6 minutes. Drain and cool in cold water. (Remove the cling film if you are using it, or the skin if you wish.)

- *To make the sauce:* sweat the vegetables in the butter for about 2 minutes, without colouring, stirring constantly. Add the white wine and reduce by half. Then pour in the fish stock and reduce by half again. Add the cream and simmer for 2 minutes. Season to taste and keep warm.

- Grill the sausages under a medium heat for 5–6 minutes, turning occasionally, until golden brown.

- Divide the sauce and vegetables between four warmed plates and place the sausages on top.

Tartar of Fresh Tuna with Seaweed

If tuna is not in season use turbot, and if you cannot find seaweed, substitute with oak-leaf lettuce.

SERVES 4

300g (*11oz*)	fillet of tuna, skinned and carefully boned
	the juice of 1 lime
	a pinch of chilli powder
4	small spring onions, finely cut
2 tablespoons	olive oil
100g (*4oz*)	seaweed (passe-pierre, perce-pierre or criste marine), blanched, refreshed and dried
1 teaspoon	parsley, finely chopped
	salt, freshly ground pepper

- Cut the tuna into 1-cm (*½-in*) pieces.

- Place the fish in a large glass salad bowl (or stainless steel bowl) and squeeze the lime juice over it. Gently lift the fish and mix it well with the juice.

- Sprinkle in the chilli powder and the spring onions and mix again. Pour over 1 tablespoon of the oil and season lightly with salt and pepper. Cover and chill in the refrigerator for at least 1 hour.

- Just before serving, dress the seaweed with the remaining tablespoon of oil, a little pepper and the chopped parsley.

- Drain the fish and transfer to a dry serving dish and serve with the seaweed salad.

Poppy Seed Mille-Feuilles with Herring Roes, Curry Butter Sauce

SERVES 4

320g (*11oz*)	soft herring roe, cleaned
1 quantity	puff pastry (see page 32)
1	egg yolk
2 tablespoons	poppy seeds
2 tablespoons	olive oil
25g (*1oz*)	butter
4	small spring onions, finely sliced at an angle
12	spinach leaves, thick stalks removed and chopped
	salt, freshly ground pepper
4	cherry tomatoes, blanched and skinned, to garnish

Curry butter sauce

1	small shallot, finely chopped
20g (*¾oz*)	butter
1 tablespoon	mild curry powder
	a pinch of turmeric
100ml (*4fl oz*)	dry white wine
100ml (*4fl oz*)	fish stock (see page 22)
100ml (*4fl oz*)	double cream
80g (*3oz*)	butter, chilled and cut into cubes
	lemon juice to taste
	salt, freshly ground pepper

- Preheat the oven to 220°C/425°F/Gas 7.

- Roll out the puff pastry 2mm (*⅛in*) thick into a rectangle approx 35 × 20cm (*14 × 8in*). Place the rectangle on a greased, dampened baking sheet. Using two forks, pierce as many holes in the pastry as possible. Leave to rest in the refrigerator for 10 minutes.

- Brush about a third of the pastry with egg yolk and sprinkle liberally with poppy seeds. Bake in the preheated oven for about 15 minutes, until crisp and light golden. Remove and when cool cut into 12 rectangles of about 5 × 7cm (*2 × 2¾in*); reserve the best four pieces with the poppy seeds for the top.

- *To make the sauce:* sweat the shallot in 20g (*¾oz*) butter until transparent. Add the curry powder and the turmeric, and then the white wine and fish stock. Bring to the boil and reduce rapidly by half.
  Add the cream and simmer for a few minutes to reduce a little more. Remove the pan from the heat and whisk in the cold butter, piece by piece. Strain through a sieve or a muslin, bring back to the boil and season with salt, pepper and lemon juice to taste. Keep warm.

- *To prepare the filling:* pat dry the herring roe and season with salt and pepper. Sauté the roe in the oil and half the butter for 30 seconds. Add the spring onion and sauté slowly for 1 minute. Remove and keep warm.
  Sauté the spinach in the rest of the butter until soft. Season with salt and pepper.

- Meanwhile, warm the pastry pieces and the cherry tomatoes in a moderate oven for a few minutes. Liquidise the sauce or work with a hand blender until light and frothy.

- To serve, place a piece of pastry on each of four warmed plates. Half cover with buttered spinach, allowing it to spill over slightly on one side. Arrange the first layer of herring roe mixture on top. Continue stacking with another piece of pastry and another layer of herring roe mixture. Finish with the last piece of pastry topped with poppy seeds.
  Pour the sauce around and garnish with a warm cherry tomato.

Note It is important that this dish is assembled at the very last minute so that the pastry remains crisp.

Grilled Squid with Olive Oil and Parsley

CALMAR GRILLÉ À L'HUILE D'OLIVE ET PERSIL

SERVES 4

900g (*2lb*)	small squid
1 tablespoon	parsley, finely chopped
15g (*½oz*)	butter, softened
2 tablespoons	olive oil
	salt, freshly ground pepper
2	lemons to garnish

- Holding the squid by the tentacles, pull off the heads and remove the insides and beaks. Cut off the tentacles below the eyes and chop them up. Loosen and pull out the quills from inside the squid, and discard the ink sacs.

- Mix the tentacles with the parsley, salt, pepper and butter. Stuff the bodies of the squid with this mixture and close the end of each squid with a wooden toothpick.

- Season with salt and pepper, brush them with olive oil and grill them, turning once, for 10–15 minutes in all.

- Arrange the squid on four plates and garnish each with half a lemon.

Note The prepared squid may be sprinkled with melted butter, lemon juice and chopped parsley. Serve with boiled potatoes.

Grilled Sea Bream
on Saffron Noodles with Basil

SERVES 4

8	pieces of sea bream, each weighing about 50g (*2oz*)
1	small shallot, finely chopped
80ml (*3fl oz*)	dry white wine
1 tablespoon	Noilly Prat
250ml (*8fl oz*)	fish stock (see page 22)
1	bunch of basil, leaves and stalks separated
200ml (*7fl oz*)	double cream
1 quantity	saffron noodles (see page 35)
10g (*½oz*)	butter
4 teaspoons	olive oil
1	tomato, blanched, skinned, deseeded and diced
	salt, freshly ground pepper
4	sprigs of basil to garnish

- *To make the sauce:* combine the shallot, white wine and Noilly Prat in a pan and reduce by half. Add the fish stock and basil stalks and reduce to a quarter of the original volume. Stir in the cream, simmer for 5 minutes and strain. Keep warm.

- Cook the noodles in plenty of boiling salted water for 2–3 minutes, until *al dente*. Meanwhile, cut the basil leaves into fine strips. Rinse the noodles in hot water, drain and toss in the butter. Mix the strips of basil into the noodles and season to taste.

- Meanwhile, pat dry the fish pieces and season them with salt and pepper. Brush with three teaspoons of the oil and grill them under a moderate heat for 3–4 minutes on each side.

- Sauté the tomato dice in the remaining oil and season.

- To serve, divide the noodles between four warmed plates and place the fish pieces on top. Spoon the sauce around, and garnish with the tomatoes and sprigs of basil.

Salt Cod with Olives

SERVES 4

600g (*1lb 5oz*)	salt cod, washed in cold water and soaked for 12 hours (change water frequently)
2	small shallots, finely chopped
2 teaspoons	white wine vinegar
40g (*1½oz*)	black olives, stoned and chopped
2	fillets of anchovy, finely chopped
1	clove of garlic, finely chopped
20g (*¾oz*)	capers, finely chopped
2 teaspoons	olive oil
	the juice of half a lemon
2 tablespoons	parsley, finely chopped
50ml (*2fl oz*)	fish stock (see page 22)
	freshly ground pepper

- Drain the cod and put it in a large saucepan with the shallots and the vinegar. Cover with cold water and bring to the boil. Simmer until tender; this will take about 50–60 minutes. Drain and leave to cool. Remove the skin and bones, and flake the fish.

- In a large bowl, mix the fish, olives, anchovy, garlic and capers. Add the oil, lemon juice and parsley. Mix carefully and moisten with the fish stock.

- Leave in the refrigerator for at least 2 hours before serving.

Note Serve with boiled rice if desired.

Steamed Sardines
with Fresh Coriander

SARDINES À LA VAPEUR AVEC CORIANDRE

Sardines in their silver skins, garnished with graceful fronds of coriander and a spoonful of this dark, glossy sauce, makes this dish one of the easiest and most successful I have ever cooked.

The scales of sardines are so soft that they can be easily removed by rubbing the fish with a cloth, and the fish may be quickly gutted and boned using tweezers.

SERVES 4

800g (1¾lb)	sardines, scaled and gutted
30g (1oz)	root ginger, peeled and cut into thin strips
2 teaspoons	lemon juice
2 teaspoons	brown sugar
2 tablespoons	soy sauce
	salt, freshly ground black pepper
	coriander leaves to garnish

- Season the sardines with salt and pepper and steam them for 4–5 minutes or until completely tender.

- Meanwhile, place the root ginger, lemon juice, sugar and soy sauce in a saucepan and bring to a simmer. Remove from the heat.

- Arrange the sardines on individual plates, spoon a little sauce over each and garnish with coriander leaves.

Note Serve with a potato and chive salad in yoghurt dressing for a quick, light and delicious meal.

Sardines in a Spicy Marinade

SARDINES MARINÉES

SERVES 4

800g (*1lb 12oz*)	sardines, scaled and gutted, heads removed
3 tablespoons	olive oil
4 tablespoons	white wine vinegar
500ml (*16fl oz*)	water
2	cloves of garlic, unpeeled and coarsely crushed
1	bay leaf
1 teaspoon	white peppercorns, crushed
1 teaspoon	coriander seeds, crushed
1	small piece red chilli, very finely chopped
2 tablespoons	coriander leaves, coarsely cut
4	small spring onions, cut into pieces
	salt, freshly ground pepper
1	tomato, blanched, skinned, deseeded and diced, to garnish

- Season the sardines with salt and pepper, inside and out, and drain well.

- Heat the oil in a pan, and sauté the sardines lightly on both sides until golden. Remove and place the fish in a flat earthenware dish, side by side.

- In a large pan, bring the vinegar and water to the boil and add the garlic, bay leaf, crushed peppercorns and coriander seeds and the chilli. Simmer for 10 minutes and then cool.

- Bring the mixture to the boil again, season with salt and pepper and pour over the sardines. Sprinkle with the coriander leaves and spring onions, cover with cling film and leave to marinate for about 4 hours.

- Serve the sardines with a little of the marinade and brown bread and butter, or drained and placed on a freshly tossed salad. Garnish with tomato dice.

Turbot Tartar

TARTAR DE TURBOT

SERVES 4

250g (8½oz)	fillet of turbot, skinned and carefully boned
6	quail's egg yolks
1 tablespoon	lemon juice
1 tablespoon	cold pressed olive oil
	salt, freshly ground white pepper
1 tablespoon	chives, finely cut
	coarsely ground white pepper
	paprika
	sea salt

to garnish (chives, coarsely ground white pepper, paprika, sea salt)

- Chop the turbot fillets finely with a sharp knife.

- Transfer to a bowl and mix with two of the egg yolks, the lemon juice and olive oil. Season carefully with salt and pepper, cover and leave in the refrigerator for about 30 minutes.

- Adjust the seasoning if necessary and arrange in rounds on individual plates (you can use a pastry cutter for this).

- Make a dent in the middle of each round of turbot and carefully place in each a quail's egg yolk. Garnish with the chives, pepper, paprika and sea salt (see photograph).

Turbot in Filo Pastry with a Champagne Sabayon Sauce

This is an unusual and effective dish. Other firm fish can be substituted for turbot, and you can include shellfish if you wish.

SERVES 4

500g (*1lb 2oz*)	fillet of turbot, skinned, carefully boned and cut into cubes
1 quantity	fish sabayon (see page 25)
4	large leaves of filo pastry (see page 33)
2 or 3	pale green leek leaves, cut into long, thin strips and blanched
40g (*½oz*)	butter, melted
100ml (*4fl oz*)	champagne
	salt, freshly ground pepper

- Preheat the oven to 190°C/375°F/Gas 5.

- Make the fish sabayon according to the instructions on page 25 and keep warm.

- Pat dry the cubes of turbot, season with salt and pepper and divide between the four sheets of filo pastry. Draw up the corners of each sheet, enclosing the fish filling, and tie carefully with a strip of leek.

- Brush well with melted butter and bake in the preheated oven for about 10 minutes.

- Finish the sauce with the champagne, liquidise or whisk with a hand blender to make the sauce light and frothy, and adjust seasoning.

- Place a turbot parcel on each of four warmed plates and serve with a little of the sauce.

Jellied Monkfish with Tomato Sauce

MÉDAILLONS DE BAUDROIE EN GELÉE, AU COULIS DE TOMATES

SERVES 4

500g (*1lb 2oz*)	monkfish tail in one piece, with bone, skinned and cleaned
30g (*1oz*)	butter
200g (*7oz*)	peeled and diced vegetables: onions, carrots, celery, tomatoes
300ml (*½ pint*)	Tokay wine (or a sweet wine)
800ml (*28fl oz*)	fish stock (see page 22)
1 tablespoon	white wine vinegar
3–4	egg whites
4	leaves of gelatine, softened in a little cold water and squeezed dry
	salt, freshly ground pepper
	salad leaves to garnish

Tomato sauce

200g (*7oz*)	tomatoes, blanched, skinned and deseeded
1 tablespoon	tarragon, finely snipped
	salt, freshly ground pepper

- Melt the butter in a large casserole and stir in the diced vegetables. Pour in about two-thirds of the wine and simmer for 2–3 minutes.

- Season the fish with salt and pepper and arrange on the vegetables. Braise, covered, for 6–8 minutes on top of the stove.

- Remove the fish and vegetables and leave to cool. Lift the flesh off the spine and chill thoroughly.

- Pour the fish stock over the vegetables and simmer for a further 3 minutes. Add the vinegar and the rest of the wine. Check seasoning. Strain and chill. Skim any fat from the surface of the stock.

- To clarify the liquid, lightly beat the egg whites and transfer to a large pan. Pour in the cold stock, bring slowly to the boil, stirring constantly, and strain.

- Stir in the softened gelatine until dissolved, and pour half the liquid into a 1.5-litre (*2½-pint*) terrine. Chill until it begins to set. Lay the fish fillet on it and cover with the rest of the jelly. Chill until set.

- *To make the sauce:* purée the tomatoes in a blender and add the tarragon. Season with salt and pepper.

- Turn out the jellied monkfish, and cut into 2-cm (*¾-in*) slices. Then, with a pastry cutter, cut each slice into a round.

- Spread the tomato sauce on four plates. Arrange the rounds on the sauce and garnish with a few salad leaves.

Note The seasoning for food to be served cold should be stronger than for hot food.

Marinated Monkfish
with Beansprouts

This is a particularly simple and appetising dish.

SERVES 4

400g (14oz)	monkfish tails without bone, skinned and cleaned

Marinade

1 tablespoon	sesame seeds, crushed
a generous tablespoon	soy sauce
	the juice of half a lemon
8	coriander leaves, finely cut
	salt, freshly ground white pepper
8	small spring onions, thinly sliced
100g (4oz)	beansprouts
1 tablespoon	olive oil
	sea salt, freshly ground white pepper

- Trim the fish and cut it into very thin slices.

- Mix together all the marinade ingredients.

- Arrange the pieces of fish on four plates and brush with the marinade. Cover and leave in the refrigerator for 15 minutes.

- Sweat the spring onions and beansprouts in the olive oil for 1½ minutes. Season.

- Remove the fish from the refrigerator and serve immediately with the hot onion and sprout mixture spooned over.

Steamed Fillet of Sea Bass with Caviar Sauce

FILET DE LOUP DE MER À LA VAPEUR, SAUCE AU CAVIAR

Sea bass is one of the finest fish and deserves a little champagne!

SERVES 4

600g (1lb 5oz)	fillet of sea bass, with skin, scaled, bones carefully removed
	salt, freshly ground pepper

Caviar sauce

50ml (2fl oz)	dry white wine
150ml (¼ pint)	fish stock (see page 22)
150ml (¼ pint)	double cream
20g (¾oz)	butter, chilled and cut into cubes
25g (1oz)	caviar
50ml (2fl oz)	champagne
	salt, freshly ground pepper

- Cut the fish fillets into four portions. Season with salt and pepper and set aside.

- *To make the sauce:* combine the white wine and fish stock in a saucepan and reduce to half their original volume by rapid boiling. Add the cream and reduce until the required consistency is obtained. Remove the pan from the heat and whisk in the butter, piece by piece. Bring back to the boil, season to taste and keep warm.

- Steam the sea bass fillets for 1½ minutes.

- Meanwhile, liquidise the sauce or whisk it with a hand blender to make it light and frothy. Gently stir in the caviar, taking care not to break up the eggs. Finish the sauce with champagne and adjust the seasoning.

- To serve, arrange the fillets on four warmed plates and spoon the sauce around.

Note This may be served with spinach and new potatoes.

John Dory Fillets without a Name

FILETS DE ST PIERRE SANS NOM

SERVES 4

4	fillets of John Dory, each weighing about 180g (*7oz*), with skin, scaled and carefully boned
20g (*¾oz*)	butter
200ml (*7fl oz*)	fish stock (see page 22)
50ml (*2fl oz*)	dry white wine
150ml (*¼ pint*)	double cream
	lemon juice to taste
200g (*7oz*)	tomatoes, blanched, skinned, deseeded and diced
1 tablespoon	olive oil
	salt, freshly ground pepper
4	sprigs of chervil to garnish

- Preheat the oven to 200°C/400°F/Gas 6.

- Season the John Dory fillets with salt and pepper and place in a well-buttered fireproof dish. Add the stock and white wine, and bring to the boil. Cover with buttered paper and poach in the oven for 4–5 minutes.

- Remove the fish and keep warm. Reduce the cooking liquid by half, add the cream and bring to the boil. Liquidise or work with a hand blender until light and frothy, add a little lemon juice to taste and adjust seasoning.

- Sauté the tomato dice gently in the oil for about 3 minutes. Season with salt and pepper.

- Place the tomatoes in the middle of four warmed plates, arrange the fillets on top and pour the sauce around. Garnish the fish with the sprigs of chervil.

John Dory Fillets with Matchstick Vegetables

FILETS DE ST PIERRE AUX JULIENNES DE LÉGUMES

SERVES 4

4	fillets of John Dory, each weighing about 200g (*7oz*), with skin, scaled and carefully boned
100g (*4oz*)	potatoes, peeled and cut into small cubes
100g (*4oz*)	fresh or 10g (*¼oz*) dried morels, soaked
50g (*2oz*)	butter
100g (*4oz*)	leeks, white part only ⎫
80g (*3oz*)	celeriac, peeled ⎬ cut into fine strips
200ml (*7fl oz*)	double cream, reduced by half
	salt, freshly ground pepper
1 tablespoon	chives, finely cut to garnish

- Cut the fillets into neat pieces. (This may not be necessary if you are using a fish with thinner fillets.) Season with salt and pepper.

- Boil the potato cubes gently in salted water until half cooked. Drain and set aside.

- Wash the morels, remove the stalks and cut in half.

- Measure 50ml (*2fl oz*) water into a saucepan, add a little salt and bring to the boil. Add the butter, morels, vegetables and the half-cooked potatoes. Place the fish pieces on top of the vegetables, cover and braise gently for 4–6 minutes. Remove the fish and keep warm.

- Stir the cream into the vegetable mixture. Check the seasoning.

- Spoon the vegetables and sauce on to four warmed plates and arrange the pieces of fish on top. Garnish with a sprinkling of chives.

  Note This recipe may be made with other firm white-fleshed fish, such as monkfish and halibut.

Red Mullet Fillets Baked in Salt

FILETS DE ROUGET À GROS SEL

SERVES 4

8	fillets of red mullet, each weighing about 60g (*2oz*), with skin, scaled and carefully boned
1 tablespoon	tarragon ⎫
1 tablespoon	chervil ⎬ snipped
1 tablespoon	rosemary, chopped
	freshly ground pepper

Salt crust

1kg (*2¼lb*)	sea salt
1	egg white
50ml (*2fl oz*)	water

- Preheat the oven to 190°C/375°F/Gas 5.

- Season the red mullet with the herbs and pepper.

- *To make the salt crust:* beat together the egg white and water and with this dampen the salt until it forms a sticky mixture.

- Spread half of this mixture on a baking tray large enough to hold the eight fillets. Place the mullet on the salt crust, skin uppermost, and cover with the remaining salt mixture.

- Bake in the oven for 8–12 minutes. Break open the salt crust and carefully remove the fillets.

- Arrange on a plate and serve.

Note A herb sauce (see page 28) may be served separately and the fish may be garnished with lemon quarters.

Baked Rolled Mackerel with Orange and Lemon Balm

PAUPIETTES DE MAQUEREAU À L'ORANGE ET À L'AMÉLISSE

Mackerel is an oily-fleshed fish which responds well to the tartness of oranges and lemons.

SERVES 4

4	fillets of fresh mackerel, each weighing about 120g (*4oz*), with the skin and tails left on, bones carefully removed

Stuffing

1	small shallot, finely chopped
25g (*1oz*)	butter
3 tablespoons	fresh white bread, crumbed
	the grated rind of half an orange
2 tablespoons	lemon balm, finely chopped
1 tablespoon	chives, finely cut
	a squeeze each of orange and lemon juice to bind the stuffing
	salt, freshly ground pepper
	the juice of 2 oranges
75ml (*3fl oz*)	dry white wine
15g (*½oz*)	butter to dot the fish
100ml (*4fl oz*)	fish stock (see page 22)
100ml (*4fl oz*)	double cream
50g (*2oz*)	butter, chilled and cut into cubes
	lemon juice to taste
	salt, freshly ground pepper
	carrot balls or cubes ⎱ to garnish
4	sprigs of lemon balm ⎰

- Preheat the oven to 190°C/375°F/Gas 5.

- *To make the stuffing:* sweat the shallot in the butter until transparent and then leave to cool. Mix the breadcrumbs with the orange rind, lemon balm and chives. Add the shallot and lightly bind together with a squeeze of orange and lemon juice. Adjust seasoning.

- Season the mackerel fillets with salt and pepper. Place an equal amount of stuffing at the wide end of each fillet and roll downwards. Secure with a cocktail stick if necessary.

- Place the rolled fish in a buttered fireproof dish. Add the orange juice and wine and put a small knob of butter on each piece of fish. Bring to the boil and then bake in the preheated oven for 8–12 minutes, depending on size. Remove the fish and keep warm.

- *To make the sauce:* transfer the cooking liquor to a saucepan, add the fish stock and reduce to a quarter of the volume. Add the cream, bring to the boil and simmer for 3–4 minutes. Remove the pan from the heat and whisk in the butter cubes, piece by piece. Bring back to the boil. Strain through a sieve or a muslin and then season with salt, pepper and lemon juice.

- To serve, place the fish on four warmed plates. Spoon the sauce around and garnish with carrot balls and lemon balm.

Ravioli with Seafood in Three Sauces

RAVIOLI DE FRUITS DE MER AUX TROIS SAUCES

This is a particularly attractive dish that is worth the extra work involved in the preparation.

SERVES 4

1 quantity	egg noodle dough (see page 34)
1 quantity	black noodle dough (see page 36)
1	egg yolk, lightly beaten

Stuffing

150g (5½oz)	pike flesh, skinned and boned, minced and chilled
	salt, freshly ground pepper
	a little cayenne and nutmeg
100ml (4fl oz)	double cream, chilled
8	scallops, diced and seasoned
100g (4oz)	fillet of Scottish salmon, skinned, carefully boned, diced and seasoned
10g (¼oz)	truffles, finely chopped (optional)

> fish mousseline

Sauces

½ quantity	tomato coulis (see page 31)
½ quantity	saffron sauce (see page 27)

Cream sauce

100ml (4fl oz)	fish stock (see page 22)
100ml (4fl oz)	double cream
	salt, freshly ground pepper

cut chives to garnish

- Make the doughs as described on the pages above and let them rest in a cool place for one hour.

- *To make the stuffing:* season the minced pike with salt, pepper, nutmeg and cayenne and place in a basin over a bowl of ice. Slowly mix in the cream, using a wooden spoon, until the fish and cream are thoroughly blended, and then press the mixture through a tamis sieve. Check seasoning.
  Combine this mousseline with the diced scallops and salmon and the chopped truffles, and check seasoning.

- Roll out the doughs to 1mm (¹/₁₆in) thick and cut into circles, 5cm (2½in) in diameter. Place a tablespoon of the stuffing in the middle of each circle of dough, brush the edges with the beaten egg yolk and fold the circles in half. Press the edges together well.

- *To make the sauces:* prepare the tomato coulis and the saffron sauce as described on pages 31 and 27. Keep warm.
  To make the cream sauce, reduce the fish stock by half. Add the cream and reduce to required consistency. Season with salt and pepper. Keep warm.

- Cook the ravioli in boiling, salted water until *al dente* (for 4–5 minutes). Drain on kitchen towel or a cloth.

- Arrange on warmed plates with a little of each sauce and decorate with chives.

Marinated Herrings

HARENGS MARINÉS

This recipe is particularly suitable for a cold buffet, served with salad, or for a first course or a picnic.

SERVES 4

1kg (2¼lb)	herrings, scaled and cleaned, heads, tails and fins removed
1 tablespoon	olive oil
150g (5½oz)	onions, finely chopped
200ml (7fl oz)	white wine vinegar
150ml (¼ pint)	water
	a few black peppercorns, crushed
	a few coriander seeds, crushed
1 teaspoon	mustard seeds
1	small bay leaf
2	sage leaves
	salt, freshly ground pepper
1	medium carrot, cut with a cannelle knife, thinly sliced and blanched for 1 minute ⎫
	a few sprigs of flat-leaf parsley ⎬ to garnish

- Rinse out the herrings with cold water and dry well with kitchen towel. Season them inside and out with salt and pepper.

- Heat the oil in a heavy pan and sauté the fish for 3–4 minutes on each side, until golden.

- Remove from the pan, allow to drain, and place in a deep dish. Scatter the chopped onion over the fish.

- Bring the vinegar, water, a little salt and all the other ingredients to the boil, allow to cool and then pour over the fish.

- Cover with cling film and marinate for about 2 hours in the refrigerator.

- Arrange the herrings attractively on a plate and serve with some of the marinade. Garnish with parsley and carrot slices.

Young Salted Herring in Onion Marinade

MATJES-HERING MARINÉ AUX OIGNONS

Matjes are the new season's young fish that have not yet reached maturity. They are caught and salted each spring, and are a choice delicacy.

SERVES 4

4	young salted herring, each weighing about 180g (*7oz*), cut into pieces and carefully boned
150ml (*¼ pint*)	milk
150ml (*¼ pint*)	soured cream
1	large onion, thinly sliced
½	green apple ⎫
½	red apple ⎬ cored and thinly sliced
	freshly ground pepper
	paprika
1 tablespoon	chives, finely cut, to garnish

- Soak the herrings for 1 hour in the milk.

- Make a marinade from the cream, onion and apple.

- Remove the fish from the milk, drain well, season with pepper and a pinch of paprika, and add to the marinade. Mix together well and allow to stand for 4 hours.

- Arrange attractively on individual plates (shape with a pastry cutter if you wish) and sprinkle with finely cut chives and a little paprika.

Note Pumpernickel or brown bread is particularly good with this dish.

Herring with Tomatoes and Mustard

DÉLICE DE HARENG AUX TOMATES ET MOUTARDE

Herring is becoming very popular again and – prepared this way – it is a delicious and healthy fish.

SERVES 4

4	herrings, each weighing about 200g (*7oz*), skinned, filleted and bones carefully removed
1 tablespoon	herb mustard
	a few thyme leaves
1	small shallot, finely chopped
60g (*2oz*)	ripe tomatoes, blanched, skinned, deseeded and diced
2 tablespoons	fish stock (see page 22)
	salt, freshly ground pepper
	a few sprigs of fresh tarragon for garnish

- Score the skin side of the fillets with a small, sharp knife at 2-cm (¾-*in*) intervals. Season with salt and pepper and rub the mustard on the inside of each fillet. Fold each fillet in half and set aside in a cool place for about 30 minutes.

- Place the herring fillets in a non-stick frying pan, sprinkle with thyme leaves and sauté for about 2 minutes on each side, until golden brown. Remove and keep warm.

- Sauté the shallot in the same pan until transparent, then add the tomatoes and stock. Season and heat gently.

- Divide the hot tomato mixture between four warmed plates and arrange the herring fillets on top. Garnish with sprigs of tarragon and serve immediately.

MAIN COURSES

Halibut Escalopes with Courgettes

ESCALOPES DE FLÉTAN AUX COURGETTES

The attraction of this dish lies in the contrast of green vegetables, the tender white flesh of the fish, and the bubbling golden sauce.

The flesh of the halibut is sliced very thinly and therefore needs very little cooking time.

SERVES 4

600g (*1lb 5oz*)	fillet of halibut, skinned, bones carefully removed (keep the skin and bones for the stock)
250ml (*8fl oz*)	fish stock (flavoured with the bones and skin of the halibut and see page 22)
100ml (*4fl oz*)	dry white wine
200ml (*7fl oz*)	double cream
2 tablespoons	double cream ⎱ mixed together
1	egg yolk ⎰ and strained
30g (*1oz*)	butter
300g (*11oz*)	courgettes, cut lengthways into 3-mm (*⅛-in*) slices and blanched
1 tablespoon	fresh white breadcrumbs
1 tablespoon	Parmesan cheese, grated
	salt, freshly ground pepper

- Cut the fish diagonally into 6-mm (*¼-in*) thick slices and season with salt and pepper. Set aside.

- Combine the fish stock and white wine in a saucepan and boil rapidly to reduce by half. Add the double cream and reduce by half again.
  Lower the heat, move the pan to the edge of the stove and carefully stir in the cream-and-egg mixture. Season to taste. Don't let the sauce cook again or it will separate.

- Brush four large flat plates with butter and sprinkle them with salt and pepper. Fold the courgette slices in half and arrange around the edge of the plates. Lay the thin slices of fish on top and coat with the sauce. Sprinkle with the breadcrumbs and the Parmesan, season with a little freshly ground pepper, and place the plates under a hot grill for about 1 minute or until golden. Serve immediately.

Fillets of Halibut with Red Onions

FILETS DE FLÉTAN AUX OIGNONS ROUGES

SERVES 4

4	fillets of halibut, each weighing about 160g (*6oz*), skinned and carefully boned
300g (*11oz*)	red onions, finely sliced
100ml (*4fl oz*)	red wine (preferably Beaujolais)
1 teaspoon	orange zest
1 teaspoon	honey
3 tablespoons	olive oil
30g (*1oz*)	butter
10g (*½oz*)	butter, melted
	salt, freshly ground pepper
4	sprigs of tarragon to garnish

- Season the fish fillets with salt and pepper and set aside.

- Place the onions and red wine in a fireproof dish and season lightly with salt and pepper. Cover and simmer until soft, stirring occasionally with a wooden spoon. Add the orange zest and honey. Keep warm.

- Heat the oil and 30g (*1oz*) butter in a frying pan and sauté the fillets on each side for about 2 minutes or until golden.

- Arrange the onions on four warmed plates, place the fish fillets on top and brush them with the melted butter. Garnish with tarragon sprigs and serve immediately.

Thin slices of Halibut, Oriental Style

ÉMINCÉ DE FLÉTAN ORIENTAL

The halibut in this recipe is simply marinated, not cooked, so it must be of a very good quality, and very fresh.

SERVES 4

450g (*1lb*)	fillet of halibut, skinned and bones carefully removed
	the juice of half a lemon
2 teaspoons	Meaux mustard
2 teaspoons	Dijon mustard
2 tablespoons	rice vinegar
150ml (*¼ pint*)	fish stock (see page 22), reduced by half and cooled
50g (*2oz*)	daikon (white radish), peeled
50g (*2oz*)	red radish
50g (*2oz*)	carrot, peeled
25g (*1oz*)	celery
25g (*1oz*)	enoki mushrooms
15g (*½oz*)	flaked almonds, toasted
	a few leaves of lamb's lettuce, washed and dried
	salt, freshly ground pepper

{daikon, red radish, carrot} cut into very thin strips and soaked in cold water

- Slice the halibut diagonally, very thinly, and season with the lemon juice, salt and pepper. Cover and leave to marinate for 5–10 minutes in the refrigerator.

- Meanwhile mix together the two mustards, vinegar and fish stock. Season well and leave to stand at room temperature until needed.

- To serve, arrange the halibut slices on plates. Mix the mustard sauce again and spoon over the fish. Garnish with the julienne of vegetables, mushrooms, flaked almonds and lamb's lettuce.

Baked Scorpion Fish

FILET DE RASCASSE AU FOUR

SERVES 4

4	scorpion fish, each weighing about 300g (*11oz*), filleted, skinned and carefully boned (keep the heads and dorsal fins)
2 tablespoons	olive oil
	the juice of 1 lemon
1	sprig of thyme
½	bay leaf
1	clove of garlic, crushed with skin
2	small shallots, finely chopped
500ml (*16fl oz*)	water
	salt and cayenne pepper

- Place the oil in a heavy saucepan, add the lemon juice, thyme, bay leaf, garlic and shallots. Add the fish heads and dorsal fins of the fish. Cover with the water, and bring to the boil; simmer gently for 10 minutes.

- Preheat the oven to 160°C/325°F/Gas 3.

- Remove the bones from the stock and strain. Reduce by fast boiling to half the original volume.

- Place the fillets in an ovenproof dish, season with salt and cayenne and add the reduced stock. Cover and poach gently for 5–6 minutes in the oven.

- Serve immediately in the cooking dish if suitable. If not, transfer the fillets to a warm serving dish and spoon over the cooking juices.

Skate Wings
with Fresh Garden Vegetables

AILES DE RAIE À LA JARDINIÈRE

This is a simple, delicious way of serving skate. The vegetables can be varied, according to season.

SERVES 4

4	pieces of skate, each weighing 250g (8½oz), with skin
1 litre (1¾ pints)	*court bouillon* (see page 23)
60g (2oz)	butter
2 tablespoons	flat-leaf parsley, chopped
	the juice of half a lemon
500g (1lb 2oz)	mixed vegetables:
	small white onions
	baby carrots, scraped
	baby sweetcorn ⎫ blanched
	parsnips, peeled and cut into strips
	broccoli florets ⎭
	mangetout peas, trimmed
	cherry tomatoes, blanched and skinned
	button mushrooms
	salt, freshly ground pepper and a pinch of sugar to taste

- Trim the fish and season with salt and pepper. Heat the *court bouillon* in a wide saucepan and gently poach the fish for 8–10 minutes.

- Meanwhile, melt half the butter in a small saucepan, and toss in it the parsley. Squeeze over the lemon juice and season lightly.

- Glaze all the vegetables, including the mangetouts, tomatoes and mushrooms; to do this, dissolve a little sugar and salt in the remaining butter in a saucepan over a medium heat and add the vegetables. Stir carefully to coat them in the butter, adding a little water if necessary. Cover and braise gently for about 2 minutes, shaking the pan to keep the vegetables moving and to prevent sticking and burning.

- To serve, place a piece of skate on each of four warmed plates and spoon over the parsley, butter and lemon juice. Arrange the vegetables attractively around the fish.

Skate au Gratin with Sherry Vinegar Sauce

RAIE AU GRATIN, SAUCE VINAIGRETTE

SERVES 4

4	pieces of skate, each weighing about 180g (7oz), blanched for 30 seconds and carefully skinned
1 tablespoon	olive oil
3	small shallots, very finely chopped
250ml (8fl oz)	fish stock (see page 22)
1 tablespoon	sherry vinegar
60g (2oz)	butter, chilled and cut into cubes
1 teaspoon	parsley, finely chopped
1 teaspoon	tarragon ⎫ finely snipped
1 teaspoon	chervil ⎭
1 teaspoon	chives, finely cut
15g (½oz)	gherkins, finely cut
15g (½oz)	capers
	salt, freshly ground pepper

- Season the pieces of fish with salt and pepper.

- Heat the oil in a non-stick pan, and put in the fish and any juices that have accumulated after blanching and skinning the fish. Sauté the fish on each side for about 3–4 minutes, depending on the thickness of the pieces. Remove and keep warm.

- *To make the sauce:* put the shallots into the same non-stick pan and add the stock and sherry vinegar. Deglaze by stirring briskly with a wooden spoon, scraping off and dissolving any sediment on the bottom of the pan. Reduce the liquid rapidly to a quarter of its volume. Remove the pan from the heat and whisk in the butter cubes, one by one. Reheat the sauce and then stir in the herbs, gherkins and capers. Season to taste.

- Meanwhile, heat the grill to a moderately hot temperature.

- Arrange the fish on warmed plates, spoon the sauce over and around the fish and pass under the preheated grill for about 1 minute to colour. Serve immediately.

Tuna Steaks Teriyaki

STEAK DE THON TERIYAKI

Sake – a Japanese 'wine' made from fermented rice – is now widely available. Mirin – a sweetened rice alcohol – is used to flavour food, and can be bought from Oriental grocers.

SERVES 4

4	fillets of tuna or tuna steaks, each weighing about 150g (5½oz), skin removed
1 tablespoon	soy sauce
3 tablespoons	mirin
3 tablespoons	sake
1 teaspoon	brown sugar
80ml (3fl oz)	fish stock (see page 22)
	salt, freshly ground pepper

- Mix the soy sauce, mirin, sake, sugar and the fish stock in a small saucepan and bring to the boil. Remove the pan from the heat.

- Arrange the fish fillets in a dish, pour over the marinade and leave for 15–20 minutes.

- Heat the grill to a moderate temperature, and grill the seasoned fish for 5 minutes on each side, brushing three or four times during the grilling with the marinade. When done, the fish should be tender and coated with a rich brown glaze.

- Serve immediately on warmed plates.

Monkfish with Mustard Sauce

SERVES 4

4	slices of monkfish tail, each weighing about 150g (5½oz) (3cm (1–1½in) thick), skinned, with bone
	flour to dust the fish

Mustard sauce

40g (1½oz)	carrots, peeled
40g (1½oz)	leeks } cut into small dice
40g (1½oz)	celeriac
20g (¾oz)	butter
150ml (¼ pint)	fish stock (see page 22)
60g (2oz)	butter, cut into cubes and chilled
1 tablespoon	Dijon mustard
1 tablespoon	flat-leaf parsley, finely chopped
1 tablespoon	olive oil
20g (¾oz)	butter
	salt, freshly ground pepper
	flat-leaf parsley to garnish

- Trim the monkfish slices. Season with salt and pepper and dust with flour. Set aside.

- *To make the mustard sauce:* in a heavy pan sweat the vegetable dice without colouring in 20g (¾oz) butter. Add the stock and reduce to a quarter by boiling rapidly. Take the pan off the heat, and quickly whisk in the butter cubes, little by little, to thicken the sauce. Stir in the mustard and the parsley. Season to taste. Keep warm.

- Heat the olive oil and the remaining 20g (¾oz) butter in a sauté pan and gently sauté the monkfish slices for 4–5 minutes each side.

- Spoon the sauce on to four warmed plates and arrange the monkfish slices on top. Serve immediately, garnished with a sprig of flat-leaf parsley.

Grilled Monkfish
with Vinaigrette Sauce

QUEUE DE LOTTE GRILLÉE À LA VINAIGRETTE

SERVES 4

4	monkfish tails, each weighing about 200g (*7oz*) with bone (160g (*6oz*) without bone), skinned
1 tablespoon	olive oil
	salt, freshly ground pepper

Vinaigrette sauce

100ml (*4fl oz*)	olive oil
50ml (*2fl oz*)	red wine vinegar
150g (*5½oz*)	ripe tomatoes, blanched, skinned, deseeded and diced
1 tablespoon	each of basil, dill and chives, cut into fine strips
10	coriander seeds, crushed
	salt, freshly ground pepper
4	sprigs of basil to garnish

- Pat dry the fish with kitchen towel and season with salt and pepper.

- *To make the sauce:* mix the olive oil and vinegar slowly. Add the tomatoes, herbs and crushed coriander seeds, and season with salt and pepper. Warm very gently over a low heat.

- Brush the fish with olive oil and then grill carefully under a preheated grill for 4 minutes on each side.

- To serve, arrange the fish on individual plates and spoon the warm sauce vinaigrette around it. Garnish with the basil sprigs.

Trout Fillets in Filo Pastry

SERVES 4

4	fillets of trout, each weighing about 100g (4oz), skinned and carefully boned
250ml (8fl oz)	lobster sauce (see page 30)
80g (3oz)	leeks, trimmed, cut into fine dice and blanched
20g (¾oz)	butter
100g (4oz)	spinach leaves, blanched and squeezed dry
100g (4oz)	mushrooms, finely chopped
8	sheets of filo pastry (see page 33)
8	long stalks of chives, blanched
	salt, freshly ground pepper

- Make the lobster sauce as described on page 30. Keep warm.

- Preheat the oven to 200°C/400°F/Gas 6.

- Cut each fillet into four pieces, season with salt and pepper, and set aside.

- Sweat the leeks without browning in the butter until just cooked; add spinach and mushrooms and season to taste.

- Arrange a little spinach mixture on each sheet of filo pastry, put two pieces of fish on top and finish with a final layer of spinach. Fold together the edges of the pastry to form parcels and bind together with the chives (see photograph).

- Place all the parcels on a greased baking tray and bake for 6–8 minutes, or until they are golden brown.

- Liquidise the lobster sauce so that it is light and frothy and divide between four warmed plates. Carefully arrange two trout packages on each plate and serve immediately.

Note You can replace the lobster sauce with a herb sauce (page 28) if you wish.

River Trout Fillets with Leeks

FILETS DE TRUITE DE RIVIÈRE AUX POIREAUX

This dish is made up of a simple blend of colours and flavours.

SERVES 4

8	fillets of trout, each weighing about 80g (3oz), skinned and carefully boned
2 teaspoons	groundnut oil
1 tablespoon	vegetable oil
15g (½oz)	butter
250ml (8fl oz)	natural, low-fat yoghurt
	a pinch of cayenne pepper
1 teaspoon	Angostura bitters
200g (7oz)	leeks, cut into very small strips and blanched
	salt, freshly ground pepper

- Season the trout with salt and pepper, sprinkle with the groundnut oil and leave to marinate for 30 minutes.

- Quickly sauté the fish fillets in the vegetable oil and butter for 1 minute each side, and leave on kitchen paper to drain. Keep warm.

- Meanwhile, in a small saucepan, combine the yoghurt, cayenne and Angostura bitters. Add the leek strips and heat gently. Check the seasoning.

- Divide the yoghurt mixture between four warmed plates and carefully place a fillet alongside. Serve immediately, with new potatoes if desired.

Salmon Trout with Mangetout and Lobster Sauce

This is a very simple and colourful dish, and it could be served with any cream sauce, such as saffron sauce (see page 27).

SERVES 4

4	fillets of salmon trout, each weighing about 150g (5½oz), with skin, carefully boned
1 quantity	lobster sauce (see page 30)
200g (7oz)	mangetout peas, trimmed, blanched and refreshed in cold water
50g (2oz)	butter
	salt, freshly ground pepper

- Make the lobster sauce as described on page 30 and keep it warm.

- Split the peas lengthways and cut into fine strips.

- Pat dry the fillets and season them with salt and pepper. Sauté gently in 40g (1½oz) of the butter for 2 minutes each side.

- Meanwhile, in a saucepan, toss the slices of mangetout in the remaining butter and season lightly.

- To serve, place a fillet on each of four warmed plates, scatter over the mangetout strips, and spoon the hot lobster sauce around.

Trout Fillets in Dezaley Wine Sauce

FILETS DE TRUITE AU DEZALEY

Dezaley wine is a Swiss, dry, delicate white wine; if you cannot obtain it, substitute another dry white mountain wine, possibly from the Savoie area in France.

SERVES 4

8	fillets of trout, each weighing about 80g (3oz), skinned and carefully boned
40g (1½oz)	leeks, thinly sliced
40g (1½oz)	celeriac, peeled and thinly sliced
150ml (¼ pint)	Dezaley wine
150ml (¼ pint)	fish stock (see page 22)
1 teaspoon	cornflour, mixed with a little cold water
100g (4oz)	butter, chilled and cut into cubes
2 tablespoons	chives, finely cut
	salt, freshly ground pepper

- Preheat the oven to 180°C/350°F/Gas 4.

- Season the trout fillets with salt and pepper. Butter a fireproof dish and put the leek and celeriac slices in the bottom. Place the fillets on top and add the wine and stock. Bring to the boil, cover with buttered paper and poach gently for 2 minutes in the oven until tender. Remove the fish and vegetables from the dish and keep warm.

- Reduce the cooking liquid by half and then add the cornflour mixture. Bring slowly back to the boil, stirring constantly, and remove the pan from the heat. Whisk in the butter, piece by piece, to finish the sauce.

- Add the chives and adjust the seasoning.

- To serve, place two fillets on each of four warmed plates and coat with the sauce.

Note Steamed or boiled potatoes should be served on the side.

Salmon in a Cream and Chive Sauce

SAUMON D'ÉCOSSE POÊLÉ À LA CRÈME DE CIBOULETTE

SERVES 4

4	escalopes of Scottish salmon, each weighing about 150g (*6oz*)
15g (*½oz*)	butter
	salt, freshly ground pepper

Cream and chive sauce

100ml (*4fl oz*)	fish stock (see page 22)
50ml (*2fl oz*)	dry white wine
1 tablespoon	Noilly Prat
1	small shallot, finely chopped
150ml (*¼ pint*)	double cream
20g (*¾oz*)	butter, chilled and cut into cubes
1 tablespoon	chives, finely cut
	salt, freshly ground pepper

- Pat dry the salmon and season with salt and pepper.

- *To make the sauce:* put the stock, wine, Noilly Prat and shallot in a pan and boil rapidly until a quarter of the volume is left.
  Add the cream and boil gently to reduce to the required consistency. Remove from the heat and whisk in the butter cubes, one by one. Strain through a fine sieve or a muslin and season with salt and pepper. Stir in the chives, bring back to the boil and keep warm. (If you wish, you can liquidise the sauce or work it with a hand blender before adding the chives, to make the sauce extra light and frothy.)

- In a non-stick, hot frying pan sauté the salmon quickly for 15 seconds in the butter, on one side only.

- Spoon the sauce on to four warmed plates and arrange the salmon on the sauce, the raw side facing upwards. Serve immediately.

Note For this dish the fish must be served pink, so sauté it on one side only (the heat of the sauce will cook the fish a little more).

Escalopes of Salmon Trout with Cranberries

ESCALOPES DE TRUITES SAUMONÉES AUX CANNEBERGES

The special flavour of the sauce comes from using stock made from the salmon bones and skin.

SERVES 4

4	fillets of salmon trout, each weighing 140g (*5oz*), skinned and carefully boned (save the skin and bones)
	sugar to taste
	the zest and juice of 1 lime (zest blanched)
50g (*2oz*)	cranberries
120ml (*4½fl oz*)	dry white wine *plus*
4 tablespoons	dry white wine
1	small shallot, finely chopped
400ml (*14fl oz*)	fish stock (flavoured with the skin and bones of the salmon; see page 22)
250ml (*8fl oz*)	double cream
60g (*2oz*)	butter, chilled and cut into cubes
	salt, freshly ground pepper

- Preheat the oven to 180°C/350°F/Gas 4.

- Heat a saucepan of water, add the sugar and lime juice and boil the cranberries for 3 minutes. Drain and set aside.

- *To make the sauce:* in a saucepan, combine 120ml (*4½fl oz*) wine and the shallot with the stock and reduce it to a quarter of the volume. Stir in the cream and bring back to the boil. Strain the sauce through a sieve or a muslin.
  Remove from the heat and whisk in the cubes of butter, piece by piece. Add the cranberries and lime zest and season the sauce to taste. Keep warm.

- Meanwhile, season the trout fillets with salt and pepper and place them in a buttered ovenproof dish. Spoon over the 4 tablespoons of white wine and cover with foil. Bake in the preheated oven for 10–12 minutes until firm but moist.

- To serve, place the fish fillets on four warmed plates and spoon the sauce around.

Warm Scottish Salmon with Olive Oil

SAUMON D'ÉCOSSE TIÈDE À L'HUILE D'OLIVE

In this Danish recipe the salmon is cooked by the steam given off from the rich milky curd, situated between the skin and the flesh. The Danes serve it with thinly sliced cucumbers, marinated for 24 hours in salted and sweetened vinegar water and then carefully dried.

SERVES 4

800g (1¾lb)	salmon fillet cut from the middle of the fish, with skin, scaled and carefully boned
1 tablespoon	olive oil
½ teaspoon	coarse sea salt
4	sprigs of chervil or dill to garnish

- Preheat the grill to a moderate temperature.

- Cut the salmon into four pieces and brush the flesh with half the olive oil. Sprinkle with a few grains of salt.

- Place the fish under the heat and grill for 2 minutes each side. When done, the skin of the fish will be crisp and the flesh just warm.

- Place the salmon on warmed plates, brush with the remaining olive oil and garnish with chervil or dill. Serve immediately with steamed potatoes, cucumbers, courgettes, or other vegetables.

Grilled Scottish Salmon with Vegetable Ragout

SAUMON D'ÉCOSSE GRILLÉ AUX LÉGUMES

SERVES 4

8	pieces of Scottish salmon fillet, each weighing about 50g (*2oz*), skinned and carefully boned
1 tablespoon	olive oil
	salt, freshly ground pepper

Vegetable ragout

40g (*1½oz*)	courgettes
40g (*1½oz*)	green peppers
40g (*1½oz*)	red peppers
40g (*1½oz*)	yellow peppers
50g (*2oz*)	aubergines, diced
20g (*¾oz*)	butter
4	basil leaves
	salt, freshly ground pepper

} deseeded and cut into dice

24	leaves of lamb's lettuce, washed and dried, to garnish

- *To prepare the ragout:* carefully sauté the vegetables in butter for 5–6 minutes in a suitable pan. The vegetables should remain fairly crisp. Cut the basil leaves into very fine strips, add to the ragout, and season to taste with salt and pepper. Keep warm.

- Meanwhile, preheat the grill to medium hot.

- Brush the salmon with olive oil, and season with salt and pepper.

- Grill carefully for 2 minutes on each side (the salmon should remain pink).

- To serve, arrange the pieces of salmon on four plates and garnish attractively with the vegetables and lettuce leaves.

Glazed Strips of Salmon with Dill

SAUMON GLACÉ À L'ANETH

SERVES 4

500g (*1lb 2oz*)	fillet of Scottish salmon, skinned and carefully boned
2 tablespoons	dill, very finely chopped
1 quantity	white wine sauce (see page 26)
2	egg yolks
	salt, freshly ground pepper

- Cut the fillets into 3-cm (*1¼-in*) thick slices. Season with salt and pepper. Arrange on plates and sprinkle with the chopped dill. Set aside.

- Make the white wine sauce as described on page 26. Off the heat, carefully beat the egg yolks into the sauce.

- Preheat the grill to a moderate temperature. Spoon the sauce over the prepared salmon slices and glaze under the grill until golden. Serve immediately.

Note This dish is good served with young asparagus or chopped spinach.

Salmon with Carrots and Turnips in Cream Sauce

MÉDAILLONS DE SAUMON D'ÉCOSSE À LA CRÈME

SERVES 4

8	Scottish salmon fillet pieces, each weighing about 50g (*2oz*), skinned and carefully boned (keep the bones for the stock)
1 tablespoon	Noilly Prat
80ml (*3fl oz*)	dry white wine
250ml (*8fl oz*)	fish stock (flavoured with the salmon bones; see page 22)
200ml (*7fl oz*)	double cream
16	baby carrots with stalks ⎫ peeled and trimmed, leaving 5mm (*¼in*) of
8	baby turnips with stalks ⎭ the stalks
20g (*¾oz*)	butter
	salt, freshly ground pepper
4	sprigs of chervil to garnish

- Season the salmon with salt and pepper and set aside.

- *To make the sauce:* combine the Noilly Prat and the white wine in a saucepan and reduce by half. Add the fish stock and reduce by half again. Pour in the cream and reduce further until the required consistency is achieved. Season with salt and pepper and keep warm.

- Steam the carrots and turnips until just tender.

- Meanwhile, gently sauté the salmon fillets in the butter for about 1 minute each side.

- To serve, divide the sauce between four warmed plates, place the salmon on top, and garnish with the steamed vegetables and the sprigs of chervil.

Note Young, tender vegetables should be chosen for this dish so that the flavours are not too strong.

Sautéed Fillet of Gilt-head Bream with Rosemary

FILET DE DAURADE SAUTÉ AU ROMARIN

SERVES 4

4	fillets of gilt-head bream, each weighing about 150g (5½oz), with skin, scaled, and bones carefully removed
1 tablespoon	olive oil
20g (¾oz)	butter
½ tablespoon	rosemary, leaves only, finely chopped
50ml (2fl oz)	dry white wine
250ml (8fl oz)	fish stock (see page 22)
1	small shallot, finely chopped
150ml (¼ pint)	double cream
1 teaspoon	lemon juice
	salt, freshly ground pepper
4	sprigs of rosemary to garnish

- Pat dry the fish, then season with salt and pepper.

- Heat the olive oil and butter in a deep frying pan and add a little of the rosemary. Sauté the fish fillets on both sides for about 3 minutes until golden, basting the fish continually with the oil, butter and rosemary. Remove the fillets and keep warm.

- Add the white wine, fish stock and shallot to the pan and reduce by half. Stir in the cream and reduce to the required consistency. Strain and then liquidise or work with a hand blender for a few minutes until the sauce is light and frothy. Stir in the remaining rosemary and season with salt, pepper and lemon juice to taste.

- Ladle a little sauce on to each of four warmed plates and place the fillets on top. Garnish with sprigs of rosemary.

Sautéed Sea Bream with Thyme, with Cream and Parsley Sauce

FILET DE DORADE POËLÉE AU THYM, SAUCE À LA CRÈME ET PERSIL

SERVES 4

4	fillets of sea bream, each weighing about 180g (6½oz), with skin, scaled, bones carefully removed
1 tablespoon	thyme leaves, picked off the stems

Cream and parsley sauce

50ml (2fl oz)	dry white wine
150ml (¼ pint)	fish stock (see page 22)
10g (¼oz)	shallot, finely chopped
150ml (¼ pint)	double cream
1 tablespoon	parsley, stalks removed
	salt, freshly ground pepper

2 tablespoons	olive oil
20g (¾oz)	butter
	salt, freshly ground pepper

- Season the fish with salt and pepper, and divide the thyme leaves between the four fillets, rubbing them into the side with the skin.

- *To make the sauce:* reduce the white wine, fish stock and shallot to a quarter of their original volume. Add the cream and parsley. Bring to the boil quickly and then purée in a blender. Season with salt and pepper and keep warm.

- Heat the olive oil and butter in a frying pan. Sauté the fillets on each side for about 3 minutes, continually basting them with the oil and butter. Remove from the pan and drain well on kitchen towel.

- Ladle the sauce on to four warmed plates and place the fish on the sauce. Serve immediately.

Sea Bream with Fennel and Tomatoes

DORADE AVEC FENOUIL ET TOMATES

This is a quick, easy and delicious way of cooking bream.

SERVES 4

1	sea bream weighing about 1.5kg (3–3½lb) or two fish each weighing about 800g (1¾lb), scaled, gutted, rinsed and dried
2	lemons, rind and pith removed ⎤ cut into
3	medium, ripe tomatoes, blanched and peeled ⎦ thin slices
	a few sprigs of dried fennel herb (optional)
½ teaspoon	fennel seeds
150g (5½oz)	fennel bulb, finely sliced
2	medium onions, finely sliced
2	cloves of garlic, crushed but unpeeled
1 tablespoon	olive oil
125ml (4½fl oz)	dry white wine
125ml (4½fl oz)	fish stock (see page 22)
30g (1oz)	fresh white breadcrumbs
	salt, freshly ground pepper

- Preheat the oven to 180°C/350°F/Gas 4.

- Season the fish with salt and pepper. With a sharp knife make three lengthways, diagonal incisions along the side of the fish, and push the slices of lemon and tomato alternately into the incisions. They should lie flat against the fish, all facing the same direction.

- Butter a fireproof dish and sprinkle with the dried fennel, or use the fine green foliage (the tuft) at the top of the fennel bulb, and the fennel seeds. Add the onions and garlic, and slices of fennel bulb.

- Carefully place the fish in the dish and brush with the oil. Add the wine and stock and bring to a simmer. Sprinkle with breadcrumbs and bake in the preheated oven for about 12–15 minutes. After 6 minutes cover the fish tail with foil as it is thinner and cooks more quickly. (To check whether the fish is cooked, using your thumb and index finger pull a dorsal fin near the head. It should come out easily.) Remove the garlic skin.

- Serve the fish immediately in the dish in which it was baked.

Baked Sea Bream with Potato Slices

DORADE AU FOUR

SERVES 4

1	sea bream, weighing about 1.5kg (3–3½lb), scaled, gutted and fins removed (leave skin on)
1	sprig of rosemary
100ml (*4fl oz*)	olive oil
2	large onions, finely sliced
400g (*14oz*)	potatoes, peeled and cut into very fine slices
2	cloves of garlic, finely chopped
300ml (*½ pint*)	dry white wine
4	tomatoes, blanched, peeled and cut into thin slices
	salt, freshly ground pepper
2 tablespoons	parsley, finely chopped, to garnish

- Preheat the oven to 200°C/400F°/Gas 6.

- Season the fish inside and out with salt and pepper and tuck the sprig of rosemary in the abdominal cavity.

- Heat 25ml (*1fl oz*) of the oil in a suitable frying pan and sauté the slices of onion until light brown. Remove from the pan and allow to drain well. Add the slices of potato and sauté until golden but only half cooked. Season with a little salt and pepper and add the garlic and the onion slices.

- Arrange the potato-and-onion mixture in a large ovenproof dish, place the fish on top and sprinkle over 50ml (*2fl oz*) of the oil, and the wine.

- Quickly sauté the tomato slices in the remaining olive oil and then arrange in the ovenproof dish with the fish and potatoes. Braise for about 20 minutes in the preheated oven. If the fish and potatoes begin to brown too much, cover with greaseproof paper that has been brushed with oil. Baste the fish occasionally with the cooking juices.

- Just before serving, sprinkle with chopped parsley. Serve in the dish in which it was cooked.

Larded Perch Fillets with Thyme

FILETS DE PERCHE PIQUÉS AU LARD

Fresh pike could be used in this recipe should perch be unobtainable.

SERVES 4

4	fillets of perch, each weighing about 170g (6oz), scaled (leave skin on) and carefully boned
100g (4oz)	lean unsmoked bacon, cut into long pieces and blanched
3 tablespoons	olive oil
40g (1½oz)	butter
2 teaspoons	thyme leaves picked from stalks
	salt, freshly ground pepper

- Pat dry the perch fillets and lard the inside (skinless side) of the fillets by making small cuts with a sharp knife and tucking in the pieces of blanched bacon. Season with salt and pepper.

- Sauté the perch in the olive oil and half the butter on both sides for about 1 minute each side, until golden, doing the inside first. Arrange on four warmed plates.

- Melt the remaining butter, add the thyme leaves, season with salt and pepper and pour over the fish. Serve immediately.

Strips of Perch Fillet
in a Nettle Cream Sauce

ÉMINCÉ DE FILET DE PERCHE

Nettles are full of goodness, containing vitamins, tannin, mineral salts and iron, and have a slightly sharp, unusual flavour.

Wear gloves to gather the nettles and pick only the tender, young leaves and shoots.

To give this dish more colour, strips of red pepper may be added.

SERVES 4

800g (1¾lb)	fillets of perch, skinned, carefully boned and cut into 1-cm (½-in) strips
2	small shallots, finely chopped
40g (1½oz)	butter
60g (2oz)	tender young nettle leaves, finely chopped
50ml (2fl oz)	dry white wine
50ml (2fl oz)	fish stock (see page 22)
150ml (¼ pint)	double cream
	salt, freshly ground pepper

- Pat dry the fish fillets and season with salt and pepper.

- *To make the sauce:* sauté the shallots in half the butter. Add the nettles and sweat carefully for one minute. Pour over the white wine and fish stock and reduce by half by fast boiling. Stir in the cream and boil until the required consistency is reached. Season and strain.

- Sauté the pieces of fish in the remaining butter for 1–2 minutes. Stir into the sauce and check seasoning. Serve immediately.

Steamed Carp with Mixed Vegetables

CARPE À LA VAPEUR AUX LÉGUMES DU MARCHÉ

SERVES 4

1	carp, weighing about 1.5kg (3–3½lb), cleaned, trimmed and scaled, *or* 4 fillets, each weighing 150g (*6oz*)
3 tablespoons	rice wine
3	small spring onions ⎫ cut into
10g (*¼oz*)	root ginger, peeled ⎭ very fine strips
1 tablespoon	sesame oil
30g (*1oz*)	bamboo shoots ⎫
20g (*¾oz*)	mushrooms ⎬ cut into very fine strips
1	medium green pepper, deseeded ⎭
1 tablespoon	light soy sauce
2 teaspoons	white wine vinegar
	a pinch of sugar to taste
1 teaspoon	cornflour, mixed with a little cold water
	salt, freshly ground pepper
2	small onions, finely sliced ⎫ for garnish
12	coriander sprigs ⎭

- Carefully make a cut on the underside of the fish and open out to remove the backbone entirely, or ask the fishmonger to do this for you.

- Blanch the fish quickly in salted water for about 2 minutes, drain and pat dry. Rub with half the rice wine, season with salt and pepper, outside and in, and place the fish in a steamer. Scatter the spring onions and ginger on top and steam for 10–12 minutes.

- Meanwhile, in a suitable pan (a wok if you have one), heat the sesame oil and add the other vegetables. Sauté, stirring constantly, for about 2 minutes. Season with the rest of the rice wine, the soy sauce, vinegar and sugar. Stir in the cornflour and bring to the boil to thicken. Remove from the heat.

- Take the fish from the steamer and arrange on a serving dish. Pour the sauce with the vegetables over the fish and garnish with spring onions and fresh coriander.

Note To make the taste of the dish more authentically oriental, replace the sesame oil with chicken fat.

Carp with Soya Shoots

GOUJONS DE CARPE AUX POIS CHINOIS

Ideally this recipe should be made in a wok. However, if you don't have one, use two pans; sauté the fish in one and the vegetables in the other.

SERVES 4

4	fillets of carp, each weighing about 150g (5½oz), with skin, scaled and carefully boned
	the juice of 1 lemon
	flour to coat the fish
4 tablespoons	peanut oil ⎱ mixed together
1 tablespoon	sesame oil ⎰
120g (4½oz)	red pepper, deseeded ⎱ cut into fine strips
40g (1½oz)	mangetout peas, trimmed ⎰
2	small spring onions, finely sliced
400g (14oz)	soya shoots
2 tablespoons	soy sauce
1 tablespoon	white wine vinegar
	salt, freshly ground pepper and sugar to taste

- Cut the carp fillets into diagonal pieces (leaving the skin on). Season the pieces with salt and lemon juice, then roll them in flour.

- Heat half the oils in the wok. Fry the fish pieces quickly. Remove and keep warm.

- Pour the rest of the oil into the wok, toss in the prepared vegetables and soya shoots. Add the soy sauce and vinegar. Stir fry for about 5–6 minutes until the liquid is reduced and the mixture starts to sizzle again. Season with salt and pepper and add sugar to taste.

- Arrange the fish and vegetables attractively on warmed plates.

Pike Fillets with Braised Onion and Paprika

FILETS DE BROCHET AUX OIGNONS ET PAPRIKA

SERVES 4

4	fillets of pike, each weighing about 150g (5½oz), skinned and carefully boned
100ml (*4fl oz*)	dry white wine
300ml (*½ pint*)	fish stock (see page 22)
300g (*11oz*)	onions, finely sliced
100g (*4oz*)	butter
1 teaspoon	paprika
250ml (*8fl oz*)	double cream
60g (*2oz*)	fresh white breadcrumbs, toasted
	salt, freshly ground pepper

- Preheat the oven to 200°C/400°F/Gas 6.

- Season the pike fillets with salt and pepper and place in a buttered ovenproof dish. Add the wine and stock and cover with buttered paper. Bring to the boil and poach in the oven until just cooked; it will take approximately 6–8 minutes depending on the size. Remove the fish and keep warm (keep the stock for the sauce).

- Meanwhile, sauté the onions in half the butter and a little water until soft and transparent. Keep warm.

- Transfer the fish cooking liquid to a pan, add the paprika, and reduce to a quarter of the volume. Add the cream and reduce again to the required consistency. Season to taste.

- Meanwhile, arrange the fillets in the grill pan; sprinkle with the breadcrumbs, dot the rest of the butter on top and grill under a high heat until golden brown.

- To serve, place the onion mixture on four warmed plates and arrange the fillets on top. Whisk the sauce with a hand blender until light and frothy, and serve separately.

Pike in a Cream Sauce with Basil

FILETS DE BROCHET À LA CRÈME ET AU BASILIC

SERVES 4

4	fillets of pike (if possible with their skin), each weighing about 170g (*6oz*), bones carefully removed
200ml (*7fl oz*)	fish stock (see page 22)
150ml (*¼ pint*)	double cream *plus*
1 tablespoon	whipped cream
1 tablespoon	lemon juice
4	sprigs of basil
	salt, freshly ground pepper

- Preheat the oven to 190°C/375°F/Gas 5.

- Season the fish fillets and place in a lightly buttered fireproof dish, skin side down. Add the stock and bring to the boil. Cover with buttered paper and poach in the oven for 5–7 minutes. Remove the fish and keep warm.

- *To make the sauce:* reduce the stock by rapidly boiling it to a quarter of its volume. Add the double cream and boil for 1 minute longer.
  Strain the sauce through a muslin and stir in the whipped cream. Season with salt and pepper and lemon juice to taste. Cut the basil into fine strips and add to the sauce.

- Ladle some of the sauce on to each of four warmed plates and carefully place the fillets on top. Serve the rest of the sauce separately.

Note Once basil leaves have been cut they discolour rapidly and should therefore be cut at the last minute.

Grilled Mackerel with Cider Sauce

SERVES 4

4	small mackerel, each weighing about 200g (*7oz*), with skin, cleaned and heads removed
25g (*1oz*)	butter, melted
	salt, freshly ground pepper

Cider sauce

200ml (*7fl oz*)	fish stock (see page 22)
200ml (*7fl oz*)	dry cider
100ml (*4fl oz*)	double cream
	a few strands of saffron
25g (*1oz*)	butter, chilled and cut into cubes
	salt, freshly ground pepper

8	pieces of apple, peeled	
	icing sugar to glaze	} to garnish
1	medium tomato, blanched, skinned, deseeded and diced	

- *To make the sauce:* combine 150ml (*¼ pint*) fish stock and the cider (save a little for moistening the fish) in a saucepan and reduce by half by fast boiling. Add the cream and the strands of saffron, and boil gently to the required consistency. Remove from the heat and whisk in the butter, piece by piece. Strain through a muslin or a fine sieve and keep warm.

- Preheat the grill to a moderate temperature.

- Score the mackerel with a sharp knife, and season with salt and pepper. Place in a buttered fireproof dish and moisten the dish with the reserved cider and the remaining fish stock, then brush the fish with melted butter.

- Grill for 7–10 minutes. Remove the fish and keep warm. At the same time, sprinkle the apple pieces with icing sugar, and grill until golden brown.

- Reheat the sauce if necessary and liquidise or work with a hand blender to make it light and frothy.

- To serve, spoon some sauce on to each of four warmed plates and place the fish on top. Garnish with glazed apple pieces and the warmed tomato dice.

Sautéed Bonito with Peas

Fresh tuna, which comes from the same family of fish as bonito, may also be used in this recipe.

SERVES 4

1kg (2¼lb)	bonito, cleaned and scaled, head, fins and tail removed
1 tablespoon	olive oil
1	clove of garlic, finely chopped
400g (14oz)	tomatoes, blanched, skinned, deseeded and diced
400g (14oz)	young peas, shelled and parboiled for 5 minutes in salted water with 1 clove of garlic and 1 sprig of parsley
	salt, freshly ground pepper
2 tablespoons	parsley, finely chopped, to garnish

- Rinse and dry the fish and cut it into 2-cm (¾-in) slices. Season with salt and pepper.

- Heat the oil in a large, shallow pan and add the garlic and the tomatoes. Sauté for 4–5 minutes. Add the fish slices and continue sautéing on a low heat, for 6–8 minutes.

- Add the parboiled peas, cover and simmer gently for a further 2–3 minutes or until tender.

- Transfer to a serving dish or four warmed plates, sprinkle with the chopped parsley and serve at once.

Grey Mullet, Chinese Style

SERVES 4

8	fillets of grey mullet, each weighing about 80g (3oz), with skin, scaled and carefully boned	
40g (1½oz)	carrots, peeled	⎫
40g (1½oz)	celeriac, peeled	
40g (1½oz)	red pepper, deseeded	⎬ cut into fine strips
40g (1½oz)	leeks	
80g (3oz)	mangetout peas, trimmed	⎭
1 tablespoon	sesame oil	
1 tablespoon	soy sauce	
1 tablespoon	rice wine	
1 tablespoon	white wine vinegar	
100ml (4fl oz)	fish stock (see page 22)	
1–2 teaspoons	cornflour, mixed in a tablespoon of cold water	
	salt, freshly ground pepper	
16	coriander sprigs to garnish	

- Trim and season the mullet fillets with salt and pepper. Steam them for 1–2 minutes.

- Meanwhile, stir fry the vegetables in the oil in a wok if you have one; otherwise use a large, heavy frying pan. Deglaze the pan with soy sauce, rice wine and vinegar. Add the fish stock and bring to the boil. Stir in the cornflour mixture and bring back to the boil to thicken. Adjust seasoning.

- To serve, divide the vegetables between four warmed plates, and arrange the fish on top. Garnish with coriander leaves.

Red Mullet Fillets with Black Olives, Tomatoes and Chervil

FILETS DE ROUGETS AUX TOMATES ET CERFEUIL

SERVES 4

4	red mullet, each weighing about 250g (8½oz), with skin, scaled, cleaned and trimmed
4 tablespoons	olive oil
80g (3oz)	black olives, stoned and chopped
200g (7oz)	tomatoes, blanched, skinned, deseeded and diced
100ml (4fl oz)	double cream
	lemon juice to taste
	salt, freshly ground pepper
1 tablespoon	chervil, torn, to garnish

- With a sharp knife, slit the fish lengthwise and open out as in the photograph opposite, removing the head and bones.

- Heat half the oil in a pan and add the olives and the tomatoes. Stir well, season and sauté gently for 3 minutes. Set aside half the olives and tomatoes in a warm place for garnish. Stir in the cream and boil gently for about 2 minutes to reduce the sauce. Liquidise or work with a hand blender to make the sauce light and creamy and season to taste with salt, pepper and lemon juice. Reheat if necessary and keep warm.

- In a frying pan, heat the remaining oil and sauté the seasoned fish for about 1 minute each side, skin side up first. (Use a gentle heat as this is a delicate fish.)

- To serve, place a fish on each of four warmed plates and spoon the sauce over and around. Garnish with the reserved olives and tomato and the torn chervil.

Baked Red Mullet with Herbs

SERVES 4

8	red mullet, each weighing about 120g (4½oz), with skin, scaled and gutted (save the livers)
2 tablespoons	parsley
1	clove of garlic ⎫ finely chopped
2	small shallots ⎭
½ tablespoon	white wine vinegar
1	sprig of thyme
1	sprig of oregano
1	bay leaf, shredded
1 tablespoon	olive oil
	the juice of 1 lemon
	salt, freshly ground pepper

- Preheat the oven to 190°C/375°F/Gas 5.

- Make several diagonal cuts along the side of each fish. Place the livers inside the fish and season with salt and pepper.

- Mix together the parsley, garlic and shallots and arrange half this mixture in a shallow ovenproof dish.

- Lay the fish on top, side by side, and sprinkle with the vinegar.

- Spread the rest of the parsley mixture on top of the fish, pushing it into the cuts along the sides. Add the sprigs of thyme and oregano and the shredded bay leaf.

- Sprinkle with the oil, cover with buttered paper and bake in the oven for 8–10 minutes.

- Just before serving, sprinkle the fish lightly with lemon juice, spoon the juices over, and return to the oven for 1–2 minutes. Serve immediately.

Steamed Grey Mullet with Lobster Sauce and Saffron Noodles

Steaming the mullet preserves the lovely silver-grey colour of the skin of this fish.

SERVES 4

8	fillets of grey mullet, each weighing about 80g (*3oz*), with skin, scaled, filleted and carefully boned
1 quantity	lobster sauce (see page 30)
1 quantity	saffron noodles (see page 27)
	a knob of butter
	salt, freshly ground pepper

- Prepare the lobster sauce as described on page 30. Keep warm.

- Season the mullet fillets and steam for 1–2 minutes, skin side facing upwards.

- Meanwhile, cook the saffron noodles in plenty of boiling salted water for 2–3 minutes until *al dente*. Drain, rinse with hot water, drain and season with salt and pepper. Toss in a knob of butter.

- Put the noodles on four individual plates, arrange the mullet on top, and spoon the hot lobster sauce around.

Baked Sea Bass with Garlic

LOTTE AU FOUR À L'AIL

SERVES 4

4	fillets of sea bass, each weighing about 200g (*7oz*), with skin, scaled and carefully boned
16	spring onions
8	small cloves of garlic, with skin, lightly crushed
20g (*¾oz*)	butter
1	sprig of thyme
2	rashers of lean smoked bacon, cut into thin strips and blanched
100ml (*4fl oz*)	poultry stock (see page 24)
200g (*7oz*)	baby turnips, peeled and blanched
1 tablespoon	flat-leaf parsley, finely chopped
	salt, freshly ground pepper
1 tablespoon	chives, finely cut, to garnish

- Preheat the oven to 200°C/400°F/Gas 6.

- Trim the fish and remove any dark, fatty bits; season with salt and pepper.

- Sweat the onions and garlic slowly in the butter in a large casserole or fireproof dish until golden brown. Add the fish fillets, thyme and bacon strips and sweat for a further 2 minutes.

- Add the poultry stock and the turnips and bake in the oven for 4–6 minutes. Stir in the chopped parsley and adjust seasoning. Remove the garlic skin.

- To serve, place a piece of fish on each of four warmed plates and spoon the vegetables and sauce around. Sprinkle with the cut chives.

Sea Bass with Fresh Tomato Sauce

LOUP DE MER AU COULIS DE TOMATES

SERVES 4

4	fillets of sea bass, each weighing about 160g (*6oz*), with skin, scaled and carefully boned
	flour to dust fish
1 quantity	tomato coulis (see page 31)
1	bunch of spring onions, cut into pieces 2.5cm (*1in*) long
40g (*1½oz*)	butter
1 tablespoon	olive oil
	salt, freshly ground pepper and pinch of sugar

- Season the bass fillets with salt and pepper and dust with flour. Set aside.

- Make the tomato coulis as described on page 31. Keep warm.

- Sauté the spring onions in half the butter and a little water until tender. Season with salt, pepper and sugar. Remove, drain and keep warm.

- Sauté the fillets in the remaining butter and oil for about 3 minutes on each side. Drain on kitchen towel.

- To serve, spoon the sauce on to four warmed plates and place the fish fillets on top. Garnish with the spring onions.

Steamed Hake Medallions with Hot Peppers

MÉDAILLONS DE COLIN À LA VAPEUR AUX PIMENTS

SERVES 4

1	hake, weighing about 1.5kg (3½lb), cleaned and skinned
½	small red chilli pepper
½	small green chilli pepper
150ml (¼ pint)	fish stock (see page 22)
60g (2oz)	butter, melted
150ml (¼ pint)	double cream
1 teaspoon	lemon juice
	salt, freshly ground pepper
	chervil leaves, shredded, to garnish

- Preheat the oven to 180°C/350°F/Gas 4.

- Carefully cut eight small medallions from the fish. Pat dry with kitchen towel and season with salt and pepper.

- Place the peppers on a hot baking sheet on the top shelf of the oven. After about 20 minutes take them out of the oven and peel them (the skin will have blistered, making them easier to peel). Alternatively you could put the pods on a fork and dip them in hot oil for a few minutes. Remove the seeds from both and cut the green chilli into very fine dice. Wash your hands carefully after handling the peppers.

- Put the fish stock and the red chilli into a liquidiser. Purée and gradually add the melted butter.

- Transfer the purée to a small pan, add the cream and the diced green chilli. Bring to the boil and season with salt, pepper and lemon juice to taste. Keep warm.

- Steam the prepared fish medallions for 2–3 minutes.

- Spoon the sauce on to four warmed plates and arrange the fish medallions on top. Garnish with the shredded chervil leaves.

Swordfish Kebabs

SERVES 4

800g (1¾lb)	swordfish steaks, skinned, boned and cut into 2-cm (¾-in) cubes

Marinade

	the juice of 2 lemons
80ml (3fl oz)	olive oil
3–4	cloves of garlic, finely chopped
1 teaspoon	ground cumin
	salt, freshly ground pepper

2 tablespoons	vegetable oil
4	ripe tomatoes, blanched, skinned, deseeded and quartered
8	small white onions, peeled and blanched

- Make the marinade by combining the lemon juice, olive oil, garlic, cumin, salt and pepper in a bowl. Mix well.

- Add the fish cubes to the marinade. Toss the pieces until they are well coated. Cover with cling film and leave in the refrigerator for about 2 hours, turning occasionally.

- Heat the grill to a moderate temperature and brush the pan well with a little of the vegetable oil.

- Drain the fish cubes (reserve the marinade). Thread the fish on to skewers alternating with the tomatoes. Set aside.

- Thread the onions on to separate skewers and brush them with the reserved marinade. Grill them for about 8 minutes, turning and basting frequently with the marinade, until brown and soft. Keep warm.

- Brush the fish skewers with oil and reserved marinade. Grill them for 5–6 minutes, turning and basting in the same way.

- Serve the kebabs immediately with some of the onions at the side of each one.

Note This dish can be served with fluffy rice flavoured with parsley.

Rolled Fillet of Sole
with Chive Sauce

PAUPIETTES DE SOLE À LA CRÈME DE CIBOULETTE

SERVES 4

8	fillets of sole, each weighing about 60g (2oz), skinned
½	red pepper ⎫
½	green pepper ⎬ blanched, skinned, deseeded
½	yellow pepper ⎭ and cut into thin strips
80ml (3fl oz)	dry white wine
1 tablespoon	Noilly Prat
1	small shallot, finely chopped
250ml (8fl oz)	fish stock (see page 22)
200ml (7fl oz)	double cream
2 tablespoons	chives, finely cut
	salt, freshly ground pepper

- Season the fillets, and roll them up with mixed pepper strips inside. Secure with cocktail sticks if necessary. Set aside.

- *To make the sauce:* combine the white wine, Noilly Prat and the shallot and reduce by half. Add the fish stock and reduce to a quarter.
Stir in the cream and let the sauce simmer for 5 minutes. Strain the sauce through a sieve or a muslin and season to taste. Liquidise or work with a hand blender until the sauce is light and creamy and then mix in the chives (save ½ tablespoon for garnish).

- Meanwhile, steam the rolled fillets for 6–8 minutes.

- To serve, ladle the sauce on to four warmed plates. Arrange the fillet rolls on top and serve immediately. Garnish with the reserved cut chives.

Sole Mousse with Lobster Stuffing and Broad Bean Sauce

MOUSSELINE DE SOLE FARCIE AU HOMARD, SAUCE AUX FÈVES

SERVES 4

Sole mousse

200g (7oz)	fillet of sole, skinned, cut into pieces and chilled
200ml (7fl oz)	double cream, chilled
	salt and cayenne pepper

Lobster stuffing

50g (2oz)	cooked lobster meat, cut into fine strips
2	large button mushrooms, cut into fine strips
20g (¾oz)	butter
2	slices of truffle, cut into fine strips (optional)
	a dash of brandy
2 tablespoons	double cream
	salt, freshly ground pepper

Broad bean sauce

1 quantity	white wine sauce (see page 26)
100g (4oz)	broad beans, blanched and skinned
25g (1oz)	butter, chilled and cut into cubes

15g (½oz)	butter	
100g (4oz)	broad beans, blanched and skinned	} to garnish
1 tablespoon	lobster eggs	

- *To make the stuffing:* sauté the mushrooms in the butter for 1 minute and then stir in the truffle and lobster meat. Add the brandy and set it alight, and then add the cream. Reduce slightly so the mixture binds together. Season to taste and leave to cool.

- *To make the mousse:* place the fillets of sole with a pinch of salt in a chilled food processor. Purée well. Add half the cream and give it a couple of quick turns.
  Remove and rub through a fine sieve into a bowl; place the bowl over ice and, using a spatula, fold in the rest of the cream, little by little. Season to taste with salt and cayenne pepper.

- Preheat the oven to 180°C/350°F/Gas 4.

- Pipe or carefully spoon the mousse into four buttered moulds, making a small hollow in the centre of each for the stuffing. Pipe or spoon the stuffing in the centre leaving a little space at the top. Level the mould off with mousse and give a gentle tap to make sure there are no pockets of air.

- Cover the moulds with buttered paper. Poach in a bain-marie in the oven for about 20 minutes, or steam for 5–10 minutes. (The mousse is done when it is just firm to the touch.)

- Meanwhile, add the beans to the prepared sauce and bring to the boil. Simmer gently for 5 minutes. Liquidise the mixture and strain it through a fine sieve if you want a smooth sauce. Return it to the pan, correct the seasoning and, off the heat, whisk in the butter cubes, piece by piece.

- Melt the remaining 15g (½oz) butter in a small saucepan and drop in the broad beans for the garnish, to warm through.

- To serve, turn the mousses out on to four warmed plates. Spoon the sauce around and garnish with the warmed broad beans and the lobster eggs.

Sole Mousse with Watercress

If you wish, you can colour and flavour some of the sole mousse with watercress. To do this, add 2 tablespoons of watercress purée (made with the leaves of half a bunch of watercress and 2 tablespoons fish stock) to one quarter of the prepared sole mousse. Pipe a thin layer of the watercress sole mousse into buttered moulds, and pipe the next layer with white sole mousse. Fill with stuffing and level off with white sole mousse.
Poach as above but serve with white wine sauce (see page 26) rather than broad bean sauce, and garnish with sprigs of watercress.

Fillets of Sole with Green Noodles

FILETS DE SOLE POCHÉS AUX NOUILLES VERTES

Lemon sole may also be used for this recipe as the sauce has a positive flavour of its own.

SERVES 4

2	Dover sole, each weighing about 500g (*1lb 2oz*), skinned and carefully filleted
1	small shallot, finely chopped
1	tomato, blanched, skinned, deseeded and diced
250ml (*8fl oz*)	fish stock (see page 22)
250ml (*8fl oz*)	dry white wine
100ml (*4fl oz*)	double cream
200g (*7oz*)	home-made green noodles (see page 35)
30g (*1oz*)	butter
	salt, freshly ground pepper

- Preheat the oven to 190°C/375°F/Gas 5.

- Flatten the fillets slightly with a knife blade and fold each one in half skin side inside. Place them in a well buttered dish and season lightly. Sprinkle the shallot and tomato on top and add the stock and white wine.

- Bring to the boil, cover with foil or buttered paper and poach in the oven for 5–10 minutes. Remove the fish and keep warm.

- *To make the sauce:* transfer the fish cooking liquid to a pan and reduce by half. Add the cream and reduce until the sauce is the right consistency. Strain the sauce and liquidise or work with a hand blender until light and creamy. Season with salt and freshly ground pepper.

- Meanwhile, cook the fresh noodles in plenty of boiling salted water for 2–3 minutes until *al dente*. Rinse quickly in very hot water, drain well, toss in the butter and season with salt and pepper.

- Arrange the noodles on four warmed plates and place the fish on top. Spoon the sauce around.

Sole Stuffed with Mixed Vegetables

SOLE FOURÉE AUX LÉGUMES

SERVES 4

4	sole, each weighing about 350g (*12oz*), cleaned, skinned and trimmed

Vegetable filling

80g (*3oz*)	courgettes	
80g (*3oz*)	carrots, peeled	diced
60g (*2oz*)	celery	
60g (*2oz*)	leeks	
40g (*1½oz*)	butter	
4 tablespoons	fish stock (see page 22)	
	salt, freshly ground pepper	

1	small shallot, finely chopped
1 tablespoon	Noilly Prat
80ml (*3fl oz*)	dry white wine
250ml (*8fl oz*)	fish stock (see page 22)
200ml (*7fl oz*)	double cream
60g (*2oz*)	fresh breadcrumbs
2 tablespoons	parsley, finely chopped
	salt, freshly ground pepper

- *To make the filling:* braise the vegetables in the butter and 4 tablespoons stock until just tender. Season with salt and pepper and keep warm.

- Preheat the oven to 190°C/375°F/Gas 5.

- Butter a large fireproof dish and sprinkle the shallot in it. Add the Noilly Prat and white wine, bring to the boil, and add the stock. Season the sole with salt and pepper and place in the dish. Cover with buttered paper and poach in the oven for 5–8 minutes. Remove the fish and carefully bone without breaking the fillets. Keep warm.

- Reduce the cooking liquid to a quarter, add the cream, and reduce again, to the required consistency. Strain, adjust the seasoning and keep the sauce warm.

- Stuff the sole fillets with the vegetables, retaining the original shape of the fish as much as possible. Preheat the grill; it should be hot, to gratinate the fish.

- Mix the breadcrumbs with the parsley and coat the fillets with the mixture. Place the fish under the hot grill for 1 minute.

- Meanwhile, liquidise the sauce or work with a hand blender to make it light and frothy, and reheat if necessary.

- Place a stuffed fish on each of four warmed plates and spoon the sauce around. Serve immediately.

John Dory Fillets with Saffron

FILETS DE ST PIERRE AU SAFRAN

SERVES 4

4	fillets of John Dory, each weighing 160g (*6oz*), skinned and carefully boned
250ml (*8fl oz*)	fish stock (see page 22)
	a few strands of saffron
1 tablespoon	Noilly Prat
80ml (*3fl oz*)	dry white wine
1	small shallot, finely chopped
200ml (*7fl oz*)	double cream
2	tomatoes, blanched, skinned, deseeded and diced
2 tablespoons	parsley, finely chopped
	salt, freshly ground pepper
4	sprigs of basil to garnish

- *To make the sauce:* first heat the fish stock in a saucepan, add the saffron strands and leave to infuse. In another saucepan, combine the Noilly Prat and white wine with the shallot, and reduce by half by fast boiling. Add the fish stock and saffron and reduce to a quarter. Then pour in the cream and simmer for 2 minutes. Strain the sauce through a muslin or a fine sieve, add the tomato dice and simmer for about 3 minutes more. Stir the chopped parsley into the sauce and season to taste with salt and pepper.

- Meanwhile, season the John Dory fillets and steam them for 3–4 minutes.

- To serve, spoon the hot sauce on to four warmed plates and place the John Dory in the centre, on the sauce. Garnish with basil sprigs.

John Dory with Red Onions

FILETS DE ST PIERRE AUX OIGNONS ROUGES

Red onions have a mild, sweet taste, and the beetroot is used here to preserve their red colour.

SERVES 4

4	fillets of John Dory, each weighing about 170g (*6oz*), skinned and carefully boned
250ml (*8fl oz*)	fish stock (see page 22)
2	tomatoes, blanched, skinned, deseeded and diced
150ml (*¼ pint*)	tomato juice
2 tablespoons	tomato paste
	a pinch of sugar
2	medium red onions, finely sliced
20g (*¾oz*)	butter
1	tablespoon honey
200ml (*7fl oz*)	red wine
20g (*¾ oz*)	raw beetroot, cut into large pieces
	salt, freshly ground pepper
4	basil leaves for garnish

- *To make the sauce:* in a saucepan, reduce the fish stock by half, then add the tomatoes, tomato juice and paste. Simmer for 5 minutes, and season with salt and sugar to taste. Blend in a liquidiser and then pass through a sieve. Keep warm.

- Sweat the onions in the butter until transparent. Add the honey, red wine and beetroot, and simmer until all the liquid has evaporated. Season, and remove the beetroot.

- Meanwhile, season the fillets of John Dory with salt and pepper, and steam them for 2–3 minutes.

- To serve, arrange the fillets on four warmed plates and garnish with the onions and basil leaves. Serve the sauce separately.

John Dory with Celery in Vinaigrette

This is a very simple dish, but do make sure that everything is to hand before cooking the fish.

SERVES 4

4	fillets of John Dory, each weighing about 150g (5½oz), skinned and carefully boned
1	medium slice of crustless white bread, cut into ½-cm (¼-in) cubes
5 tablespoons	clarified butter for sautéing
1	stick of celery, sliced thinly at an angle
25g (1oz)	carrot, peeled, cut into very thin slices and blanched for 1 minute
4 tablespoons	olive oil
1 tablespoon	white wine vinegar
	the juice of half a lemon
3	ripe tomatoes, blanched, skinned, deseeded and puréed
	salt, freshly ground pepper
	chervil or celery leaves to garnish

- Preheat the oven to 190°C/375°F/Gas 5.

- Cut the John Dory fillets into thin slices at an angle, season with salt and pepper and place in a buttered ovenproof dish. Cover and keep in a cool place until required.

- Sauté the bread cubes in the clarified butter until golden brown, and drain on kitchen towel.

- Combine the celery, carrot, oil and vinegar, and season to taste.

- Season the fish with a squeeze of lemon and sprinkle with water. Bake in the oven for 3–4 minutes.

- Warm the tomato purée in a small saucepan.

- To serve, divide the vegetable salad between four plates and lay the fish pieces on top. Season the fresh tomato purée and spoon over the fish. Scatter over a few croûtons and garnish with chervil or celery leaves.

Turbot with Shrimp and Mussel Sauce

FILET DE TURBOT AUX CREVETTES ET MOULES

SERVES 4

4	fillets of turbot, each weighing about 170g (*6oz*) skinned and bones carefully removed
25g (*1oz*)	shrimps or prawns, lightly cooked and peeled
16	mussels, soaked, scrubbed and beard removed
100ml (*4fl oz*)	water
200ml (*7fl oz*)	fish stock (see page 22)
1	small shallot, finely chopped
100ml (*4fl oz*)	dry white wine
200ml (*7fl oz*)	double cream
1	egg yolk
20g (*¾oz*)	butter, chilled and cut into cubes
	salt, freshly ground pepper

- Wash the mussels thoroughly and discard any that are broken or that float during cleaning. Put the water, half the fish stock and the mussels in a pan and bring to the boil. Boil until the mussels open – it will take about 3–4 minutes – and throw away any that have not opened. Remove from the shells and set aside.

- Butter a large fireproof dish, add the shallot, and place the seasoned turbot on top in a single layer. Add the white wine and remaining fish stock. Cover, bring to the boil and simmer for 4–6 minutes until the fish is firm and white. Remove the fillets and keep warm.

- Boil the cooking liquid rapidly to reduce it to a quarter of its original volume. Add 150ml (*¼ pint*) of the cream and boil a further 5 minutes. Remove the pan from the heat, mix the remaining cream with the egg yolk, strain and stir into the sauce. Whisk in the butter a little at a time and then strain the sauce through a fine sieve or a muslin. Season to taste and bring back to a simmer. Do not boil or it will curdle.

- Heat the grill to moderately hot.

- Place the turbot fillets on warmed plates and arrange the shrimps and mussels on top. Spoon over the hot sauce and place under the grill for about 1 minute. Serve at once.

Turbot in Mushroom Crust, Red Wine Sauce

SERVES 4

4	fillets of turbot, each weighing 125g (*5oz*), skinned and carefully boned

Mushroom crust

1	small shallot, finely chopped
50g (*2oz*)	butter
100g (*4oz*)	button mushrooms, finely chopped
	the juice of half a lemon
40g (*1½oz*)	fresh wholewheat breadcrumbs
1 tablespoon	fresh herbs (thyme, dill, parsley), finely chopped

Red wine sauce

200ml (*7fl oz*)	fish stock (see page 22)
150ml (*¼ pint*)	red wine
100ml (*4fl oz*)	red port
2	small shallots, finely chopped
100ml (*4fl oz*)	double cream
100g (*4oz*)	butter, chilled and cut into cubes

salt, freshly ground pepper
mustard and cress to garnish

- Preheat the oven to 220°C/425°F/Gas 7.

- *To make the crust:* sweat the shallot slowly in half the butter for about 5 minutes. Add the mushrooms and a squeeze of lemon juice. Sauté quickly for 1–2 minutes. Season to taste. Drain off any excess juice and keep aside.
  Add the breadcrumbs, herbs and the rest of the butter. Mix gently and taste again for seasoning.

- Lightly season the fish fillets with salt and pepper, and coat the top of each with the mushroom mix. Place in a buttered ovenproof dish and add the fish stock for the sauce. Bake in the hot oven for 5–8 minutes. Remove the fillets and keep warm.

- *To make the sauce:* reduce the cooking liquid with the wine, port and shallots to one quarter of its volume. Add the cream, bring to the boil and simmer for 2 minutes; then whisk in the cold butter, piece by piece, off the heat.
  Strain through a fine sieve or a muslin, liquidise or work with a hand blender until light and frothy, and correct seasoning.

- To serve, spoon the sauce on to four warmed plates and place the fish on top. Garnish with mustard and cress.

Turbot Fillets in Cabbage Leaves with Pepper Sauce

FILET DE TURBOT EN HABIT VERT

You can use green peppers to make a green sauce to replace the yellow sauce if you wish.

SERVES 4

4	fillets of turbot, each weighing about 150g (5½oz), skinned and carefully boned
4	Savoy cabbage leaves or lettuce leaves, blanched quickly in salted water and refreshed
½ quantity	yellow pepper sauce (see page 29)
½ quantity	red pepper sauce (see page 28)
400ml (14fl oz)	fish stock, for steaming (see page 22)
	salt, freshly ground pepper

- Season the turbot fillets with salt and pepper. Wrap half of each fillet with a cabbage leaf and set aside.

- Make the sauces as described on pages 28 and 29, and keep warm.

- Steam the prepared fish over the fish stock for about 3–4 minutes.

- Reheat the two well-seasoned sauces if necessary and spoon carefully on warmed plates. Place the fish fillets on top.

Warm Turbot with Black Truffles

MÉDAILLONS DE TURBOT TIÈDE AUX TRUFFES NOIRS

SERVES 4

4	fillets of turbot, each weighing about 150g (5½oz), skinned and carefully boned
20g (¾oz)	butter
220ml (8fl oz)	fish stock (see page 22)
	a few strands of saffron
100ml (4fl oz)	double cream
2 tablespoons	olive oil
½ tablespoon	white wine vinegar
4	leaves oak-leaf lettuce ⎱ washed and
	a little curly endive ⎰ carefully dried
10g (¼oz)	black truffles, sliced and cut into fine strips
	a few leaves flat-leaf parsley
	a few chives
	a pinch of paprika
	salt, freshly ground pepper

- Season the fish with salt and pepper, and set aside.

- Melt the butter in a fireproof dish and add 60ml (2fl oz) of the fish stock. Bring to the boil, add the fish fillets and cover with buttered paper. Poach gently for about 3 minutes or until just cooked. Lift out the fish and set aside.

- Add the saffron strands and the remaining stock to the dish and reduce to a sixth of the original volume. Then add the cream and boil gently to reduce by half. Strain through a fine sieve or a muslin, season, and leave to cool a little.

- Blend the olive oil and the vinegar and season to taste. Dress the salad leaves with this vinaigrette.

- To serve, place the warm fish on four plates and garnish with the strips of truffle and the parsley. Spoon a little saffron sauce on to each plate and arrange the salad leaves and chives attractively. Finish with a dusting of paprika.

Note When the turbot has poached leave it to cool a little: it is a gelatinous fish and delicious when eaten just warm.

Stewed Octopus

POULPE À LA MARSEILLAISE

SERVES 4

800g (1¾lb)	octopus, cleaned and cut into small pieces
3 tablespoons	olive oil
1	small leek, diced
4	medium tomatoes, blanched, skinned, deseeded and diced
	a few strands of saffron
1	medium onion, finely chopped
1	clove of garlic, crushed
	a bouquet garni of thyme, fennel, bay leaf and celery
150g (5½oz)	long-grain rice, washed and drained
	salt, freshly ground pepper
2 tablespoons	parsley, finely chopped, to garnish

- Pat dry the octopus pieces with kitchen towel and season with salt and pepper. Heat the oil in a fireproof casserole. Toss in the octopus pieces and sauté over a brisk heat until golden brown.

- Add the leek, and as soon as the leek starts to colour, add the tomatoes, saffron, onion and garlic. Add enough water to cover the contents of the casserole by about 1cm (½in). Add the bouquet garni. Cover and simmer over a low heat for 1 hour, adding water from time to time to keep the level of the liquid constant.

- Stir in the rice, season and, keeping the pan covered, cook over a low heat for a further 20 minutes.

- Serve straight from the casserole, or in a heated serving dish. Sprinkle with chopped parsley.

Note Cooking time for the octopus will vary according to the size and age of the octopus. Squid may be used in this recipe instead of octopus.

Baby Octopus and Fennel in Wine

SERVES 4

700–800g (1½–1¾lb)	baby octopus, cleaned (see page 17)
2 tablespoons	olive oil
250ml (8fl oz)	dry red wine
300ml (½ pint)	fish stock (see page 22)
3–4	small tomatoes, blanched, skinned, deseeded and diced
2 tablespoons	fennel herb, finely cut
4	small spring onions, finely cut
	salt, freshly ground pepper
1 tablespoon	parsley, finely chopped, to garnish

- Cut the octopus tentacles into rounds, the thickness of a little finger. Pat dry with kitchen towel and season with salt and pepper.

- Heat the oil in a saucepan and add the octopus. Sauté for 4–5 minutes until lightly coloured.

- Add the wine and deglaze the pan, stirring and dissolving any deposits on the bottom of the pan. Add the fish stock, tomatoes and fennel and braise, covered, for about 45 minutes. (Check from time to time and if necessary add a little more fish stock.)

- Add the spring onions and season to taste.

- To serve, arrange in a serving dish or on individual warmed plates and sprinkle with chopped parsley.

Note The braising time of the octopus can vary, depending on the size and the age of the octopus; it should be cooked until 'fork tender'.
This dish is equally delicious served cold.

Squid Stuffed with Rice and Pine Nuts

The squid in this recipe is braised in tomato sauce; alternatively it can be poached in well-seasoned fish stock for about 45 minutes, or steamed for about 20 minutes (as in the photograph opposite).

SERVES 4

4	squid, each weighing about 200g (7oz), cleaned, tentacles cut off and reserved

Stuffing

1	large onion, finely chopped
1 tablespoon	olive oil
100g (3½oz)	long-grain rice
80g (3oz)	pine nuts
40g (1½oz)	currants
2 tablespoons	parsley, finely chopped
	salt, freshly ground pepper
2 tablespoons	olive oil
3	medium tomatoes, blanched, peeled, deseeded and diced
400ml (16fl oz)	tomato juice
100ml (4fl oz)	medium dry white wine
	salt, freshly ground pepper
	basil sprigs to garnish

- Preheat the oven to 180°C/350°F/Gas 4.

- Rub the squid with salt to remove the skin and rinse well in running water. Pat dry.

- *To make the stuffing:* sauté the onion in the oil until transparent. Add the rice, pine nuts, currants and parsley and season with salt and pepper. Mix well.

- Partially fill the squid with the stuffing, leaving room for the rice to swell. Close up the openings with wooden cocktail sticks. Season with salt and pepper.

- Heat the oil in a frying pan and over a high heat sauté the stuffed squid and the tentacles for about 2 minutes. Arrange them in a fireproof casserole.

- Add the tomatoes, tomato juice and wine. Season with salt and pepper.

- Cover the casserole and braise in the preheated oven for about 45 minutes or until the squid are tender and the sauce is thick. If necessary, add more tomato juice.

- Remove the squid and tentacles, and then strain the tomato sauce through a sieve.

- Arrange the squid and tentacles on four warmed plates, with a spoonful of sauce and a sprig of basil.

Note This dish is delicious served hot or cold, perhaps with a ratatouille.

Poached Eel in Green Sauce

ANGUILLE POCHÉ, SAUCE VERTE

SERVES 4

1.2kg (*3lb*)	eel, skinned, gutted and cut into 3-cm (*1¼-in*) pieces
1 tablespoon	lemon juice
400ml (*14fl oz*)	fish stock (see page 22)
150ml (*¼ pint*)	dry white wine
100g (*4oz*)	turnip, peeled and sliced
3 tablespoons	parsley stalks
100g (*4oz*)	onion, roughly cut
1	bay leaf
10	white peppercorns, lightly crushed
1 teaspoon	juniper berries, lightly crushed
20g (*¾oz*)	butter
1 teaspoon	plain flour
1	egg yolk } whisked together
80ml (*3fl oz*)	double cream } and strained
2 tablespoons	dill } finely cut
4	leaves sage }
	salt, freshly ground pepper and sugar to taste

- Dry the eel pieces with kitchen towel and season with salt and pepper. Sprinkle the lemon juice over the fish, cover and leave for 15 minutes.

- In a saucepan, bring the fish stock and the wine to boiling point. Add the turnip, parsley, onion, bay leaf, peppercorns and the juniper berries, and simmer for 10 minutes. Season with salt, pepper and sugar to taste.

- Put the pieces of eel into the stock and poach gently for 5 minutes. Remove, cover with a damp cloth and keep warm. Leave the stock until cold. Strain.

- Melt the butter in a pan, add the flour and cook for a minute stirring constantly. Gradually add 250ml (*8fl oz*) of the cold poaching liquid and mix well until smooth. Simmer for 5 minutes and then remove the pan from the heat.

- Mix the egg-and-cream mixture into the sauce. If you wish, you can whisk the sauce at this point with a hand blender to make it light and frothy. Season to taste, add the herbs and stir in the eel pieces. Take care that the sauce does not boil again or it will separate. Serve immediately.

Barbecued Eel Kebabs, Japanese Style

SERVES 4

900g (*2lb*)	eel, skinned, gutted, boned and cut into 4-cm (*1½-in*) pieces
80ml (*3fl oz*)	sake
2 tablespoons	honey
3 tablespoons	soy sauce
	a piece of root ginger, measuring about 1cm (*½in*) square, peeled and finely chopped
1	small onion, layers separated and cut into 2-cm (*1-in*) pieces
1 tablespoon	groundnut oil
100ml (*4fl oz*)	natural yoghurt
1½ tablespoons	coriander leaves, finely cut
	salt and paprika

- In a saucepan, gently heat the sake, honey and soy sauce. Add the fresh ginger and pour the mixture over the eel pieces. Cover and leave to marinate in the refrigerator for 6 hours.

- Remove the eel and pat dry (reserve the marinade). Thread the eel on to skewers, alternating with onion pieces, and brush with oil. Season lightly with salt and paprika.

- Grill over charcoal for about 8 minutes, turning frequently.

- Meanwhile, to make the sauce, mix half the reserved marinade with the yoghurt and coriander.

- To serve, arrange the kebabs on warmed plates and spoon the sauce around. Dust with paprika.

Grilled Eel with Yellow Lentils

ANGUILLE GRILLÉE AUX LENTILLES JAUNES

SERVES 4

800g (1½–1¾lb)	eel, skinned, gutted and cut into pieces 4–5cm (1½–2in) long

Marinade

50g (2oz)	carrots ⎱ peeled and cut into dice
30g (1oz)	celeriac ⎰
1	small shallot, finely chopped
1	small clove of garlic, crushed
200ml (7fl oz)	dry red wine
2	sprigs of thyme
20g (¾oz)	butter
150g (5½oz)	yellow lentils, soaked in water overnight
300ml (½ pint)	white poultry stock (see page 24)
1 tablespoon	sherry vinegar
1 tablespoon	walnut oil
	salt, freshly ground pepper
3 tablespoons	parsley, finely chopped, to garnish

- Place the eel pieces in a deep dish. Season with salt and pepper.

- Mix together the marinade ingredients, and pour over the fish. Cover with cling film and allow to stand in the refrigerator for 24 hours.

- Remove the pieces of eel, the carrots and the celeriac and dry on kitchen towel.

- Melt the butter in a large saucepan and sweat the vegetables for 2–3 minutes. Drain the lentils and add them and the stock to the vegetables. Season and simmer slowly for about 25 minutes until soft. Stir in the sherry vinegar and check seasoning. Keep warm.

- Brush the eel pieces with the walnut oil and grill under a moderate heat for 3 minutes each side.

- Arrange the lentils on a plate and place the pieces of eel on top. Garnish with chopped parsley.

Pollan Fillets Provençal

FILETS DE POLLAN PROVENCAL

SERVES 4

600g (*1lb 5oz*)	fillets of pollan, skinned, and bones carefully removed
200ml (*7fl oz*)	beer
30g (*1oz*)	butter
3	small shallots, finely chopped
1	clove of garlic, finely chopped
4	tomatoes, blanched, skinned, deseeded and diced
25g (*1oz*)	black and green olives, stoned and cut into thin strips
100ml (*4fl oz*)	red wine
1	sprig of basil
2 tablespoons	olive oil
	flour to dust the fillets
	salt, freshly ground pepper

- Place the fish fillets in a dish, add the beer and leave to marinate for 15 minutes.

- Meanwhile, heat the butter in a pan, add the shallots and the garlic, and sauté until transparent. Add the tomatoes and simmer for a few minutes more.
  Stir in the olives, red wine and basil, and continue to simmer for 8–10 minutes. Adjust the seasoning and keep hot.

- Remove the pollan from the beer marinade and dry with kitchen towel. Season with salt and pepper and then coat lightly with flour.
  Heat the oil in a frying pan and sauté the fish fillets for 2–3 minutes each side until golden.

- Arrange the pollan fillets on four warmed plates. Spoon over the hot sauce and serve immediately.

Note This dish may be prepared with other white fish such as hake or pike. If you prefer a mild garlic flavour, leave the garlic clove whole and remove before serving.

Coral Trout Baked in its own Juices

This is a delicious way of sealing in the flavour and juices of the fish and vegetables. Open the parcels at the table so that the aroma can be fully appreciated.

It is equally successful made with roasting bags (see photograph opposite), aluminium foil or greaseproof paper, as below.

SERVES 4

4	pieces of coral trout, each weighing about 160g (*6oz*), with skin, scaled and carefully boned
50g (*2oz*)	butter, softened
25g (*1oz*)	root ginger, peeled and finely sliced
50g (*2oz*)	carrot, peeled and finely sliced
4	spring onions, trimmed
8	pieces of Chinese mushroom, soaked
4	cherry tomatoes, blanched and skinned
1 tablespoon	olive oil
	salt, freshly ground pepper

- Preheat the oven to 180°C/350°F/Gas 4. Season the pieces of fish with salt and pepper.

- Cut four pieces of greaseproof paper three times the size of the pieces of fish, butter them and place a piece of fish in the middle of each sheet of paper. Arrange the vegetables and the tomatoes on and around the fish and put a little knob of butter on each fillet. Fold and tuck under the edges of the paper to make air-tight parcels.

- Place the parcels on a greased baking sheet and bake in the oven for 7–10 minutes. Serve immediately.

Bluefish with Cabbage and Bacon in Butter Sauce

SERVES 4

4	fillets of bluefish, each weighing about 160g (*6oz*), with skin, scaled, and carefully boned

Butter sauce

2	small shallots, finely chopped
100ml (*4fl oz*)	dry white wine
200ml (*7fl oz*)	fish stock (see page 22)
4 tablespoons	double cream
150g (*5½oz*)	butter, chilled and cut into cubes
	the juice of half a lemon
	salt and cayenne pepper

2	rashers smoked streaky bacon, cut into tiny strips
25g (*1oz*)	butter
200g (*7oz*)	white cabbage, hard core removed and finely sliced, blanched and dried
1 teaspoon	white wine vinegar
1 tablespoon	parsley, finely chopped
1 tablespoon	tarragon, finely snipped
150ml (*¼ pint*)	red wine, reduced to 1 tablespoon
	salt, freshly ground pepper

- Cut each fillet in half and season with salt and pepper. Arrange in a steaming basket.

- *To make the sauce:* combine in a saucepan the shallots, white wine and fish stock and reduce to a quarter of its volume by fast boiling. Add the cream, bring back to the boil and boil gently to reduce by half again.
  Remove the pan from the heat and whisk in the butter, piece by piece. Season to taste with lemon juice, salt and cayenne. Strain through a fine sieve or a muslin, bring back to a simmer and keep warm.

- Sauté the bacon in the butter for 2–3 minutes and then add the cabbage. Moisten with the vinegar and a tablespoon of water and braise until *al dente*. Season to taste. Toss in the fresh herbs.

- Meanwhile, steam the fish for about 3 minutes.

- Stir the reduced red wine into 50ml (*2fl oz*) of the sauce to make a contrasting sauce. If you wish, liquidise the butter sauce or work with a hand blender to make it light and frothy.

- To serve, arrange a bed of cabbage and bacon on each of four warmed plates and place the fish on top. Spoon the butter sauce around and finish with a swirl of red wine sauce. Serve immediately.

Brill with Mustard in Vegetable Coats, Cream Sauce with Chives

BARBUE A LA MOUTARDE, ENROBÉ DE LÉGUMES, SAUCE À LA CIBOULETTE

SERVES 4

4	fillets of brill, each weighing about 150g (5½oz), skinned and carefully boned
1 teaspoon	Dijon mustard
1	medium daikon (white radish), peeled
2	medium carrots, peeled
2	medium yellow courgettes
2	medium green courgettes
25g (1oz)	butter, melted
	salt, freshly ground pepper

(daikon, carrots, yellow courgettes, green courgettes) sliced very thinly lengthwise and blanched

Cream sauce with chives

1	small shallot, finely chopped
100ml (4fl oz)	dry white wine
50ml (2fl oz)	Noilly Prat
200ml (7fl oz)	fish stock (see page 22)
150ml (¼ pint)	double cream
	lemon juice to taste
25g (1oz)	butter, chilled and cut into cubes
2 tablespoons	chives, finely cut
	salt, freshly ground pepper

4	radishes, cut into strips or rounds, to garnish

- Preheat the oven to 200°C/400°F/Gas 6.

- Take the four fish fillets and cut each piece in half lengthwise. Season lightly and smear the top with mustard. Wrap four pieces of the fish with alternate, crosswise strips of daikon and carrot. Wrap the remaining four pieces of fish in the same way, using the yellow and green courgettes.

- Brush all the fish parcels with melted butter and place in a buttered ovenproof dish. Moisten with a little of the white wine and the fish stock from the sauce ingredients.

- *To make the sauce:* combine the shallot, white wine and Noilly Prat in a saucepan and reduce by half. Add the fish stock and reduce by half again.
  Add the cream and simmer gently for 5–8 minutes to the correct consistency. Strain the sauce through a sieve or a muslin; adjust the seasoning with salt, pepper and lemon juice. Whisk in the butter, piece by piece, off the heat and then bring back to the boil. Liquidise the sauce, if you wish, to make it light and frothy and then stir in the chives.

- To serve, divide the sauce between four warmed plates and arrange the fillets on top. Garnish with warmed radishes and serve immediately.

Kedgeree

The Hindi Khichri, a rice and lentil dish embellished with fish or meat, was turned into the splendid kedgeree by the English in India.

SERVES 4

200g (*7oz*)	smoked Finnan haddock, with skin
200g (*7oz*)	prawns, cooked in their shells
200g (*7oz*)	fresh Scottish salmon, with skin, scaled
600ml (*1 pint*)	boiling water
4 teaspoons	olive oil
1	large onion, finely chopped
150g (*5½oz*)	basmati or other long-grain rice
1 teaspoon	curry paste or powder
20g (*¾oz*)	butter
2	eggs, hard-boiled, peeled and sliced
20g (*¾oz*)	parsley, finely chopped
	salt, freshly ground pepper

- Shell the prawns, saving four unshelled for decoration.

- Put the shells into a large saucepan and place the haddock on top. Add the boiling water, cover, and leave for 10 minutes on a low heat.

- Remove the haddock and poach the salmon in the liquid until just cooked, remove and set aside with the haddock. Continue to simmer the stock with the prawn shells.

- Skin the haddock and salmon and remove all bones. Drop the skin and trimmings into the stock pot.

- Mix the fish with the prawns, and season carefully with salt and pepper. Set aside.

- In a large pan, heat the oil and sauté the onion until golden. Stir in the rice and when it is transparent, add the curry paste or powder.

- Strain over the cooking stock, cover and simmer over a very low heat for 18 minutes until the rice is tender and the stock absorbed.

- Mix in the prepared fish and prawns, and enough butter to make the kedgeree moist. Adjust the seasoning, and heat through.

- Arrange in a warm dish or on individual plates. Place the sliced egg on top and sprinkle with parsley. Decorate with the reserved, warmed prawns and serve at once.

Grilled Mixed Fish

PANACHE DE POISSON

SERVES 4

120g (4½oz)	fillet of Scottish salmon	with skin, scaled,
120g (4½oz)	fillet of sea bass	bones carefully removed and
120g (4½oz)	fillet of red mullet	each cut into 4 portions
120g (4½oz)	fillet of sole	skinned, bones carefully removed
120g (4½oz)	fillet of turbot	and each cut into 4 portions
4 tablespoons	dry white wine	
1 tablespoon	Noilly Prat	
1	small shallot, finely chopped	
250ml (8fl oz)	fish stock (see page 22)	
200ml (7fl oz)	double cream	
	a few strands of saffron	
1 tablespoon	olive oil	
	salt, freshly ground pepper	
25g (1oz)	leek, cut into diamonds, blanched	
25g (1oz)	carrot, peeled, cut with a cannelle knife and thinly sliced, blanched	to garnish
	a few chervil leaves	

- *To make the sauce:* combine in a saucepan the white wine, Noilly Prat and shallot. Reduce by half. Add the fish stock and reduce by half again. Pour in the cream, add the saffron strands and simmer for 5 minutes. Strain through a muslin or a fine sieve, season and keep warm.

- Pat dry the fish fillets with kitchen towel and season them. Brush with oil and grill on both sides until just cooked.

- Liquidise the sauce or work with a hand blender until light and frothy.

- Warm the carrot and leek garnish in a little fish stock.

- Arrange a little sauce on each of four warmed plates and place the fish on top. Garnish with the warmed leeks and carrots, and chervil leaves.

Lasagne with Shellfish in a Chervil Sauce

LASAGNE DE FRUITS DE MER, SAUCE AU CERFEUIL

SERVES 4

320g (*11oz*)	shelled and lightly cooked shellfish (shrimps, cockles, mussels, scallops)
1 quantity	saffron noodle dough (see page 35)
200ml (*7fl oz*)	white wine sauce (see page 26)
4	sprigs *plus* 4 tablespoons finely snipped chervil
200g (*7oz*)	spinach leaves, stalks removed, roughly chopped, blanched and well drained
20g (*¾oz*)	butter
	flour for dusting
	salt, freshly ground pepper

- Make the saffron noodle dough and leave to rest for about 2 hours. Roll out as thinly as possible and cut into four sheets.

- Prepare the white wine sauce as described on page 26.

- Cut each pasta sheet in two. Place the four sprigs of chervil at even distances, in the centre of two of the sheets. Place the other two sheets on top and roll separately through a pasta machine or by hand with a rolling pin to flatten further, to the original size of the sheets. Divide each in two again.
  Cook the pasta in plenty of boiling, salted water for about 3 minutes until *al dente*. Drain and dry on kitchen towel.

- Meanwhile, heat the white wine sauce and liquidise or work with a hand blender until light and frothy. Add the shellfish and stir in the snipped chervil. Check seasoning.

- Sauté the spinach in the butter for 2–3 minutes, and then season well with salt and pepper.

- Quickly reheat the pasta sheets in salted boiling water, and dry. Arrange a single layer on four warmed plates. Spread the spinach over this and then cover with the shellfish sauce. Place the second, final layer of pasta on top and serve immediately.

Fricassée of Seafood

FRICASSÉE DE FRUITS DE MER

I have used squid, scampi, scallops and lobster here, but you can use whatever seafood is available.

SERVES 4

8	small squid, each weighing about 50g (2oz)
8	scallops in their shells
8	scampi, shelled
1	lobster tail, cooked and cut into eight pieces
1	small shallot, finely chopped
100ml (4fl oz)	dry white wine
50ml (2fl oz)	Noilly Prat
100ml (4fl oz)	fish stock (see page 22)
300ml (½ pint)	double cream
	lemon juice to taste
4	mangetout pea pods, trimmed and cut into fine strips ⎫
25g (1oz)	red pepper, deseeded and cut into fine strips ⎬ blanched
25g (1oz)	samphire ⎭
25g (1oz)	butter
	salt, cayenne and freshly ground pepper

- Holding the squid by the tentacles, pull off the heads; remove the insides and quills. Cut off the tentacles and slice if necessary. Rinse well and cut the squid into small rings.

- Open the scallop shells with a small strong knife (if necessary, place the scallops in a warm pan to open completely). Remove the scallops and corals carefully with a soup spoon, and slice the scallops horizontally in two. Trim the coral. Wash quickly and season.

- *To make the sauce:* combine in a saucepan the shallot, white wine and Noilly Prat and reduce by half. Add the fish stock and reduce to one quarter of its volume. Add the cream and simmer for 5 minutes. Strain through a sieve or muslin into a clean saucepan. Season with salt, cayenne, pepper and lemon juice.

- Bring the sauce back to a simmer and add first the seasoned scampi and the squid. Let these simmer for a minute before stirring in the scallops. Simmer for a further 30 seconds and then add the lobster pieces. Add the vegetables and check seasoning. Finish by stirring in the butter.

- To serve, arrange the seafood on a warmed serving dish or on individual plates with the sauce and garnish.

Fish and Chips

The fish can be marinated for about 30 minutes before use with lemon juice, salt and pepper, and, if you wish, a touch of garlic.

SERVES 4

600g (*1lb 5oz*)	white fish (haddock, cod, sole, plaice), skinned and cut into 4 pieces
900g (*2lb*)	potatoes, peeled
	beef dripping or vegetable oil for deep frying
	flour for dusting fish
	salt, freshly ground pepper

Batter

110g (*4oz*)	strong plain white flour
80g (*3oz*)	cornflour
1	egg, separated
280ml (*9fl oz*)	water
	a pinch each of salt and sugar, and freshly ground pepper
1 tablespoon	parsley, finely chopped

- *To make the batter:* sieve the flour and cornflour into a large bowl. Mix together the egg yolk and the water and incorporate into the flours; beat to a smooth batter. Whisk the egg white until stiff, and then fold into the batter. Season with salt, sugar and pepper, and stir in the parsley.

- Chip the potatoes to the size and shape you prefer and dry on kitchen towel.

- Heat the fat in a deep fat fryer to 150°C/300°F and blanch the chips in it until almost tender. Remove and drain, and heat the oil to 170°C/340°F.

- Season the fish, dust with flour and dip in the batter. Blanch in the hot fat for 2 minutes. Drain, keep warm, and heat the oil to 190°C/375°F.

- Refry the chips and then the fish until golden, drain thoroughly on kitchen towel and serve immediately in newspaper cornets.

Glossary of Fish and Shellfish

Anchovy
ENGRAULIS ENCRASICOLUS
Anchois

Brief Description Small, slim, round sea fish of herring family. Green-blue-black with brilliant silvery sides, a projecting upper jaw and large mouth. Measures an average 9–15cm (3½–6in) and weighs 10–30g (½–1oz).
Peculiarities Swims in shoals and is fished at night, being attracted to the fishermen's lights. When caught, its green colour turns mackerel blue, then black as it becomes less fresh.
Where Found Coastal world wide; used to be very prolific – and best – in Mediterranean, but pollution has taken a toll.
Quality Oily white flesh with aromatic taste when freshly caught. Seldom available fresh in countries where not caught. Most often anchovies are filleted and preserved by salting, brining, pickling, or marinating.
Preparation Sauté when fresh, or serve simply marinated on seafood platters. When preserved, they are an aromatic addition to butters, mayonnaises and other sauces, and soups. They are basis of many famous relishes and are made into Anchoiade, and are essential in Salade Niçoise, *Pissaladières* and many Italian pizzas.

Bluefish
POMATOMUS SALTATOR
Tassergal

Brief Description Round sea fish belonging to pompano and horse mackerel family. Streamlined with a blue-grey shine on a grey body; maximum length 100cm (40in).
Peculiarities A predatory fish so ferocious that it has been called 'the bulldog of the ocean'.
Where Found Deep waters of Atlantic and Mediterranean, but moves towards coastal areas of Europe and USA in summer.
Quality Rich, oily fish with firm flesh when very fresh.
Preparation Grill, barbecue, bake in sauces and *en papillote*. Cook like mackerel and herring, with tart accompanying sauces. Sauté small bluefish.

Bonito
SARDA SARDA
Bonite (à Dos Rayé)

Brief Description The Atlantic bonito is marine, round, a larger relative of and similar shape to the mackerel, and of same family as the tuna, the Scombridae. Has lateral stripes on upper back and measures up to 70cm (27in). The Oceanic, Californian or Pacific bonito – the skipjack – is a small species of tuna, with lateral stripes on belly; called by the French *bonite à ventre rayé* and is common in Japan as *Katsuwo*.
Peculiarities Family are oceanic fish, swimming in large shoals, and performing lengthy migrations.
Where Found In surface waters of all the temperate and tropical waters of the world.
Quality Rich, oily flesh with, some say, a texture like veal.
Preparation Grill as steaks or *en brochette*, oven-braise or bake. Bonito are also salted.

Bream, Black Bream
SPONDYLIOSOMA CANTHARUS
Griset, Brème, Dorade Grise

Red Bream
PAGELLUS CENTRODONTUS
Dorade Commune

Gilt-head Bream
SPARUS (or CHRYSOPHRYS) AURATA
Daurade

Sea Bream, Couch's Sea Bream
PAGRUS PAGRUS
Pagre Commun

Brief Description The many varieties of sea bream belong to the family Sparidae, and most can be identified by their stocky bodies, Roman noses, and one long fin down the back. There are red, grey-black, blue and golden varieties of up to 1.6kg (3¼lb) in weight, and up to 50–60cm (20–24in) in length. The forms above are those which are best known – and most gastronomically rated – in Europe. The red is grey or red-grey with a large black spot on the shoulder; the black is dark grey with golden horizontal stripes on the flanks, and very small crowded teeth; the gilt-head has a gold spot on each cheek and a crescent-shaped spot between its eyes; and the sea bream has white tips to its tail. In the USA, breams are known as porgies. There is a freshwater European bream which is related to the carp.

Peculiarities Most of the bream have grinding rather than sharp teeth as they usually live on shellfish. The gilt-head bream is found in saltwater lakes as well as the open sea, and was once sacred to Aphrodite.

Where Found Mediterranean and southern European Atlantic. The red and black are the only members of the family which come as far as northern Europe. Other varieties throughout the world.

Quality Red and gilt-head bream are considered the best, with lean, firm, white meat. A bream of Japanese waters is so good that it is eaten raw in *sashimi*.

Preparation Braise in the oven, bake, grill or poach. If filleted, serve with sauces.

Brill
SCOPHTHALMUS RHOMBUS
Barbue

Brief Description Flat fish resembling the turbot, but more oval in shape, and without knobs on the top grey or light chestnut skin. Average length 30–60cm (12–24in), weight up to 4.5kg (10lb). Primarily a sea fish, though occasionally found in river estuaries.

Peculiarities The brill is sinistral, like the turbot (majority of other flat fish are dextral). Hybrids with turbot occasionally occur.

Where Found Mediterranean and Black Seas, in Atlantic and north to Scandinavia.

Quality Flesh is not so delicate, white or firm as that of the turbot, but still good and much less expensive. Especially appreciated in France and Belgium.

Preparation As turbot, but with plainer sauces. Also grill, bake, or cut into slices and deep-fry.

Carp
CYPRINUS CARPIO
Carpe

Brief Description The several varieties of this freshwater round fish include typical carp (large strong scales), mirror carp (few scales), and leather carp (practically scaleless). Carp can be easily bred artificially (mirror and leather varieties in particular). Backs are dark green to green-brown and undersides are golden yellow; there is a pair of barbels at the mouth. They measure 20–30cm (8–12in), and weigh 1–3kg (2–4½lb). Roach, dace, chub, tench and bream are members of carp family.

Peculiarities Introduced to Europe – possibly from China – in Middle Ages. They are long-lived fish – some have been known to survive for at least 50 years – and in ponds in parks can become very tame (another relative is the goldfish).

Where Found Still or slow-moving fresh water in many parts of world.

Quality Lean, tasty white flesh; cultivated carp (of which mirror is best) have fewer bones. Put live carp taken from stagnant water in fresh water for a day or two to avoid a muddy taste. If dead, soak after scaling, etc., in mildly salted or acidulated water.

Preparation Cook *'bleu'*, stuff, sauté, poach, bake, stew, steam, or serve with sauces. There are carp specialities in many cuisines – those of Hungary, Germany, Poland and China – and carp is a Christmas Eve celebratory dish in many European countries. Soft carp roe is considered a delicacy.

Clam, Carpetshell Clam
VENERUPIS DECUSSÀTA
Palourde

Clam, Golden Carpetshell
TAPES GEOGRAPHICA
Clovisse

Clam, Warty Venus
VENUS VERRUCOSA
Praire

Brief Description Marine bivalve molluscs of which there are thousands of forms; edible ones come in both hard- and soft- (fragile-) shelled varieties. Shells are round, marked with visible concentric rings. The *palourde* is largest of the gastronomically rated European clams, reaching 7.5cm (3in), although the Smooth Venus can reach 12.5cm (5in). American Great West Coast Clam can weigh over 2kg (4½lb). The *palourde* is pale yellow to grey, with brown stripes, and the Golden Carpetshell is recognisable by its golden yellow or pink flesh. The Warty Venus has a deeply ridged shell, with wart-like spines on the margins.

Peculiarities Clams live buried in sand or mud, usually in inshore waters, and filter food particles through their bodies. Can be poisonous if they have been feeding in polluted waters.

Where Found Warm waters world wide, in Pacific, Atlantic, Mediterranean. Cultivated in France and Britain; particularly prolific in North American waters, where there is also a freshwater variety.

Quality Tender meat, and a fine flavour.

Preparation *Palourdes* and *praires* are eaten raw like oysters, as are the smallest American hard-shell clams (*Mercenaria mercenaria*). Cherrystone are about 7.5cm

(3in), Littlenecks about 6cm (2½in), and the largest, about 11cm (4½in), are the ones most used in the famous American clam chowder. Clams may also be baked, steamed, stuffed, and used in soups and sauces – the most famous of the latter being *spaghetti con vongole*.

Cod, Salt Cod
GADUS MORHUA
Cabillaud, Morue

Brief Description Lean, large, round deep-sea fish with large head and long barbels; olive green or brown back with yellow and brown spots; whitish stripes on the sides forming an arch over pectoral fins and continuing in a straight line to tail. Measures from 80–150cm (32–60in), and weighs from 3–10kg (6–22lb) (though can grow to 36kg (80lb). Its relatives, of family Gadidae, are whiting, haddock, hake, pollack, coley.

Peculiarities Major valuable food fish of countries bordering on Atlantic. Young cod are codling or scrod, and can be caught in inshore waters. Cod are voracious indiscriminate predators, and they shoal at breeding times. They have also been the cause of a 'cod war'!

Where Found Arctic Ocean from Murmansk and Greenland, North Atlantic to north coast of Spain, North Sea, Baltic Sea, Gulf of Bothnia, east coast of the USA. Also west coast of Canada.

Quality Lean, delicate, firm flesh. Good liver, from which a very nutritious oil is obtained.

Preparation Cut into fillets, slices or steaks and sauté, steam, bake, braise or grill, or poach a tailpiece whole. It is also sold dried and salted. Cod's roe is available uncooked and boiled, or smoked, when it is often used to make a kind of *taramasalata* (more genuinely made with grey mullet roe).

Common Crab, Edible Crab
CANCER PAGURUS
Tourteau, Crabe

Spider Crab
MAJA SQUINADO
Araignée

Brief Description There are thought to be over 4000 species of crab in the world, most of which are edible; two most widely found in Europe are: Common or Edible Crab and Spider Crab. Former is red-brown with smooth, oval shell and two powerful claws; it can measure well over 20cm (8in); turns bright red when cooked. The spider is pink-brown, with a very spiny, rounder shell and much smaller claws; its *maximum* length is 20cm (8in).

Peculiarities Edible crabs are very aggressive, attacking when disturbed, and can eat each other. Crabs and lobsters both moult their shells; in the waters around Venice and Chesapeake Bay, varieties are caught when new shell is tender, and served as soft-shell crabs, when virtually the whole creature can be eaten.

Where Found Both types are found in Mediterranean and Atlantic, but huge variety of crabs is eaten world wide.

Quality Delicious, useful meat; often sold cooked, but best to buy live and cook at home. Buy those that feel heavy for their size, with legs firmly attached to body: male is better for white meat (it has larger claws), but in summer female has coral which may be eaten.

Preparation Boil, dress, serve in pâtés, soups, cold as salad, potted.

John Dory, Dory
ZEUS FABER
Saint Pierre, Dorée, Jean Doré, Paule de Mer

Brief Description Oval plate-shaped sea fish with big head and large eyes. Thick skin, yellow or grey-brown, with very small scales; on flank are round blackish marks surrounded by grey circles. Top dorsal fins are nine spines held together by membrane ending in filaments. Dory is thought to come from the French *dorée*, referring to the colour. Females are bigger than males, but maximum weight is 8kg (18lb); more usual size is 5.5kg (about 12lb).

Peculiarities Very thin, and looks as if it should be a flat fish, but swims vertically and not very well: as a result, it has an ingeniously extensible jaw which thrusts out from the body to catch prey. The dorsal spine filaments grow longer as fish ages.

Where Found Mediterranean, and Atlantic Ocean up to Norway. Rare in British waters.

Quality Lean, fairly firm white flesh, similar to that of turbot, and thought by many to have an exquisite taste. High wastage when cleaning (approximately 70%) because of enormous head – but this is good for soups and stocks.

Preparation As for brill, turbot or sole, especially with creamy or egg sauces. In *bouillabaisse* or other fish soups, bake in oven or grill.

Eel
ANGUILLA ANGUILLA
Anguille

Brief Description A freshwater, snake-like fish, with slippery skin which, depending on age and where fish are found, can vary from yellow and green to brown, black and silver. Females measure up to 100cm (40in), males up to 50cm (20in); usual weight between 700g (1½lb) and 5kg (11lb). Two marine eels, the conger and the moray, belong to different but related families, and are also edible and not so rich.

Peculiarities Freshwater eel has fascinating life cycle; European and North African eels are spawned in Atlantic Ocean, somewhere to south-east of Bermuda, an area known as the Sargasso Sea; the larvae take three years to drift in the Gulf Stream to the coast and estuaries of Europe and North Africa. The elvers (*civelles*) then wriggle their way up rivers, creeks, and streams – even crossing wet fields – to reach fresh waters where they will mature for up to twelve years. Then they change colour (from yellow to silver) and shape, and make their way back to the sea in the autumn. They take six months to reach the Sargasso Sea where they spawn and presumably die (*mature* eels are never seen to make their way inland). Eels in America, Japan and Australia spawn and grow similarly.

Where Found All types of fresh water around world; Atlantic, Mediterranean and Black Seas.

Quality Fine, delicate fatty flesh which can be difficult to digest if eaten in excess; best is from fully mature eels fresh from the river on their way back to the sea. Buy them live, and cook as soon after killing as possible (eels wriggle for quite a while after death). The tail piece is full of bones.

Preparation Bake or grill mature eels, or use in ragouts or stews. Also jellied – once an East London speciality – and smoked. Elvers are deep-fried or baked, a seasonal speciality of many countries, particularly Spain and Belgium.

Haddock
MELANOGRAMMUS AEGLERINUS
Aiglefin, Eglefin

Brief Description Round sea fish of cod family, with greyish or purple-black back and a black stripe along the sides (which distinguishes it from the cod, with its *white* stripe), a black spot on sides below front dorsal fins, and barbel on its lower lip. Average length 40–60cm (16–24in); weighs from 800g–2kg (1¾–4¼lb).

Peculiarities The young, together with horse mackerel and whiting, often protect themselves from predators by staying close to jellyfish.

Where Found Deep waters in Arctic Ocean, both sides of the Atlantic, and the North Sea.

Quality White, tender, firm flesh with pleasant flavour, often considered superior to cod, and good liver. Roe is considered a delicacy.

Preparation Bake, steam, sauté, or deep-fry. Often smoked in UK, particularly Scotland. Finnan haddock is fish split and cold smoked on the bone until yellow. Arbroath smokies are small whole fish hot smoked until brown.

Hake
MERLUCCIUS MERLUCCIUS
Merlu, Colin

Brief Description Round sea fish of the cod family, with scaly, silver-grey skin, pointed head with a protuberant lower jaw, and large mouth. Average length 40cm (16in), though it can reach beyond 100cm (40in). Varieties found all over world.

Peculiarities A voracious fish with very sharp teeth, which gorges itself at night on pilchards – or its own young.

Where Found Both sides of Atlantic, from Iceland to North Africa, and in coastal Mediterranean waters. Related species occur off Canadian and Chilean Pacific coasts, and off South Africa.

Quality Fine, white flesh, closer grained and less flavoursome than cod. Flesh is easily bruised and does not keep well. The least fatty and the easiest to bone and digest of cod family, so good for invalids and children.

Preparation Poach, bake, steam, sauté, grill, stuff. Also used raw in *ceviche*, and dried, as *merluche*.

Halibut
HIPPOGLOSSUS HIPPOGLOSSUS
Flétan

Brief Description Largest of the flat fish, with grey-brown elongated body, and, in older fish, a blackish upper side. Dextral, 4.5 metres (about 15 feet) and up to 600kg (1320lb). Young halibut (chicken halibut) can weigh 500g–3.6kg (1–8lb). Several varieties, including Pacific halibut, Greenland halibut (black halibut in Germany and France). Californian halibut is sinistral, therefore more closely related to brill and turbot. Expensive.

Peculiarities Long-lived and predatory, taking codling and similar small fry.

Where Found Deep waters of the North Atlantic and Pacific Oceans, in North Sea and Arctic Ocean.

Quality Firm, tasty white flesh, coarser than that of turbot or brill. It can be dry, so moisten during cooking. A good liver, which gives an oil rich in Vitamin D.

Preparation Slice or fillet, and poach. They can also be smoked.

Herring
CLUPEA HARENGUS
Hareng

Brief Description Round sea fish with slender body, short dorsal fins and big round eyes; back is sea-green and sides have a silver shimmer. They measure

20–30cm (8–12in), and weigh 80–250g (3–9oz). Sprat, anchovy, pilchard, sardine and smelt are same family. A most important food fish.

Peculiarities Feed on small crabs, snails, fish larvae and young fish. Distinguished according to age: *matjes* are virgin herrings in which roe has not yet formed; adult herring are caught before spawning, with both milt or roe; and spent herring are thin after spawning.

Where Found North Atlantic to Scandinavia (largest herrings), in the North and Baltic Seas (smallest herrings), North Pacific.

Quality Firm, brown, oily and bony flesh (a good source of Vitamins A and D and many essential oils). Quality depends on time of year.

Preparation Fresh or 'green' herring are best simply sautéed or grilled; marinated herring are popular in Scandinavia, and smoked, dried, salted or pickled herring come in vast variety. Rollmops and Bismarck herring are raw marinated fillets; *matjes* are slightly salted and fermented and eaten raw; bloaters are ungutted cold-smoked fish, a speciality of Norfolk; buckling are German version, but hot smoked; and kippers are split, gutted and cold smoked. Herring roes, both hard and soft, are cheap and nutritious.

European Lobster
HOMARUS VULGARIS
Homard

Spiny Lobster
PALINURUS ELEPHAS
Langouste

Brief Description The two main forms of lobster common in Europe are the European and the spiny. Family includes smaller but similar creatures – crawfish or crayfish, shrimps. The European is a rich dark blue-black, smooth shelled, has eight legs and two pincers or claws; it turns red when cooked; generally about 60cm (24in) in length. The spiny (also known as crawfish in the UK and rock or southern lobster in the US) is speckled pink or brown, with a knobbly spiny shell, has ten legs, no claws and two very long antennae; generally about 50cm (20in) long.

Peculiarities Lobsters are scavengers, eating decayed rotted material (like their small cousins, the shrimps). They are able to regenerate lost limbs.

Where Found European: in the colder waters of northern hemisphere (Scottish lobsters are greatly prized), but as far south as the Mediterranean, North Africa, and North Carolina in the US. Spiny: warmer coastal waters of Atlantic, Mediterranean, Pacific and Caribbean, and South Africa, Brazil, Australia, New Zealand.

Quality The European lobster is generally accepted to have the best flavour; one of about 450–675g

(1–1½lb) is sweetest. Hen lobsters are considered more delicate than cocks; hens are broader round the tail (under which they may carry eggs or coral which is also eaten), and have a band of flesh in the head, not in the male. This, plus the greenish tomalley or liver of both sexes, is also eaten. The tails only of the spiny lobster are eaten, and these are what are frozen and generally sold as 'crawfish tails'.

Preparation Boil, grill, serve cold, or hot in sauces.

Mackerel
SCOMBER SCOMBRUS
Maquereau

Brief Description Round sea fish, distant relative of tuna and Atlantic bonito; elongated, scaleless, dark green to steely-blue body, vertically striped with crooked black lines. Average length 30–40cm (12–16in); weighs 150–250g (5–9oz).

Peculiarities A voracious fish that travels in huge shoals, feeding on smaller fish; it in turn is eaten by larger fish and by seagulls. It is believed to fast in winter.

Where Found Both sides of Atlantic, in Pacific, and in Mediterranean and Black Sea.

Quality Oily, tasty and highly nutritious flesh which can deteriorate quickly due to the oil becoming rancid. The bones are easily removed.

Preparation Poach, braise, bake, sauté, grill, stuff. Often served with sharp sauces (like gooseberry or sorrel) to counteract oily richness. Made into pâté, soused in UK, pickled in white wine in France, salted and dried in the East Mediterranean, and hot smoked.

Monkfish, Anglerfish
LOPHIUS PISCATORIUS
Lotte (de Mer), Baudroie, Gigot de Mer

Brief Description Cartilaginous deep-sea scaleless fish. Large and with an enormous, ugly toad-like head with a feeler or filaments (this is why the tail pieces only are offered for sale in shops and markets). Upper body is dark brown, underside is light. They can measure up to 2 metres (6½ feet).

Peculiarities A predator, the monkfish lies camouflaged on the sea bed and 'fishes' for its food by dangling the filaments on its head over its huge open mouth (thus the name, generally American, of 'anglerfish'). Even rays and small sharks can be thus entrapped as they swim 'in' to investigate. The monkfish is often confused with the angel fish or angel shark.

Where Found Mediterranean and Black Sea, Atlantic Ocean from the Mediterranean to Iceland and Finland.

Quality Excellent, delicate non-flaky white flesh. The

only bone is the strong spine which is easily removed; and the fish usually comes skinned.

Preparation A large amount must be allowed per person when buying, because of high water loss. Poach, roast, steam, bake, cut into steaks and sauté or grill, or grill *en brochette*. Also used in stews, and *bouillabaisse*. Can be served cold.

Mullet, Grey
MUGIL CEPHALUS
Muge, Mulet Gris

Brief Description Elegant sea fish with grey, large-scaled back, darker stripe on sides (in US called striped or black mullet), and silvery white underside. Average length 30–50cm (12–20in), weight up to 4kg (8¾lb). Family is the Mugilidae (100 species around world); they are unrelated to the smaller red mullet.

Peculiarities Essentially coastal fish, living on mud and weed; some swim up estuaries and tidal harbours (known as *cochons de mer*, sea pigs, in France), some live in saltwater lakes. They have a very long gut to cope with their herbivorous diet.

Where Found East Atlantic coasts up to south of England, and in USA. In Mediterranean and Black Sea. Related species occur in tropical waters of the Pacific.

Quality Firm, white, slightly fatty, tasty flesh, but less good than red mullet. Can taste muddy, thus should be carefully cleaned and soaked if necessary in acidulated water before cooking.

Preparation Braise whole in the oven or bake *en papillote*, fry, grill or poach and serve with a flavourful sauce. Roe used to make genuine *taramasalata* and also salted, pressed and dried as *boutargue*, a similar roe pâté.

Mullet, Red
MULLUS BARBATUS and SURMULETUS
Rouget de Roche

Brief Description Two varieties of this round sea fish in Europe: *M. barbatus* has a reddish colour and two barbels attached to point of lower jaw; measures maximum 25cm (10in). *M. surmuletus* is larger, up to 40cm (16in), with stripes on first dorsal fin and may have horizontal yellow stripes.

Peculiarities Other species known on eastern side of Atlantic are nicknamed goatfish because of the barbels. Also often known as woodcock of the sea (*bécasse de mer*, attributed to Brillat-Savarin), because they can be cooked without gutting. The scales are very fragile.

Where Found *M. barbatus* in Mediterranean only. *M. surmuletus* in Mediterranean, Atlantic, sometimes in summer as far up as southern Norway. Related species in Caribbean and Indo-Pacific seas.

Quality White, firm, delicate and lean flesh, with distinctive flavour. Fillets contain small sharp bones. The liver is considered a great delicacy.

Preparation Because it secretes no bile, the French do not bother to gut the fish before cooking. If it is gutted, the liver is left in or used for sauces. Grill, bake in foil, or sauté. Marinate and serve cold. Considerable loss of flavour when it is poached.

Mussel
MYTILIS EDULIS or GALLOPROVINCIALIS
Moule

Brief Description Marine bivalve oval mollusc, commonly blue-black, although larger yellowish ones are found in Spain (and one in New Zealand is bright green). Mediterranean mussels (*M. galloprovincialis*) are larger than those farmed in the Atlantic, as *bouchots*, and are sharper along the edges.

Peculiarities Mussels attach themselves to posts, rocks, piers, and to the ropes of modern mussel farms by their beards. They can, like clams, be poisonous from polluted waters, and can cause allergy.

Where Found In most seas, but particularly around the coasts of Europe. Less common in the USA.

Quality Tender, tasty and highly nutritious flesh containing calcium, iodine, iron and few calories (and indeed was once known as 'the poor man's oyster'). The best are the small ones from France, although those from Holland and Denmark are good as well.

Preparation They can be eaten raw, but are more usually briefly cooked steamed in a single layer for about 5 minutes for the most famous mussel dish, *moules marinière*. They can be steamed, then stuffed and briefly baked with garlic butter, or marinated and served cold. They can be grilled *en brochette*, wrapped in bacon, or sautéed.

Octopus
OCTOPUS VULGARIS
Poulpe, Pieuvre

Brief Description Varieties of this eight-legged cephalopod mollusc are found in all temperate waters throughout the world. The common octopus is best-known species, making the best eating. Reddish brown, with a large body, two eyes, and eight tentacles. Measures up to 3 metres (120in), but considered best when less than 37.5cm (15in).

Peculiarities They have no backbone and, unlike other cephalopod molluscs – squid and cuttlefish – they prefer to crawl rather than swim. They live in holes and crevices, and feed on shellfish; they in turn are eaten by moray and conger eels. Usually quite shy, though larger ones can be aggressive.

Where Found World wide.

Quality The only really tender octopus are the smaller ones. The bigger ones are beaten after being caught to soften them, but they still have to be cooked considerably longer.

Preparation Grill or sauté small octopus; boil, deep-fry or stew bigger octopus. They are dried in Tunisia.

Oyster
OSTREA EDULIS, CRASSOSTREA
Huître

Brief Description Three most common varieties (of at least 300) are *Ostrea edulis*, the Common, European or Flat oyster (the Native in Britain), Portuguese or Ports (*Crassostrea angulata*), the American (*Crassostrea virginica*). The common oyster is oval to rounded, with rough, jagged shell layers making up the top rounded side; the Portuguese is more elongated in shape.

Peculiarities Oysters cultivated by Romans in Britain at Colne and Colchester. Once cheap and abundant in Britain, food of the poor in London, they are now much rarer and more expensive. Native oyster retains its gritty eggs in its shell during summer months (the ones without an R); Ports and American oyster do not retain their eggs, thus can be eaten virtually all year round. Members of a related species occasionally hold pearls!

Where Found In all waters around the world except for the polar seas: around Europe, in Mediterranean, the Atlantic and Pacific coasts of America, and around Japan, China, Australia and New Zealand.

Quality Flavour and texture of sweet tender flesh depends on type and waters in which they are reared. Flat oysters known by place or origin; the French claim theirs are the best: the Belons (from the river Finistère), the Arcachons (from the Arcachon basin), the Marennes (from near Rochefort) and the Isigny oysters and Bretons from northern France. The English make similar claims for their Colchesters and Whitstables, the Irish for their Galway Bays, the Dutch and Belgians for their Seelands and Ostends, and the Americans for their Olympias and Bluepoints! Ports are cheaper, and less rated than common oysters.

Preparation Best eaten raw but can be cooked very briefly by simply warming through. Once included in steak and kidney puddings in their prolific heyday in Britain.

Perch
PERCA FLUVIATILIS
Perche

Brief Description Round, freshwater, deep-bodied fish with about five vertical stripes. Has two dorsal fins, the first of which is spiny; the ventral and anal fins are red. Back is greenish, the underside yellowish white, but colour depends on habitat. Average length 15–35cm (6–14in), weight 2–2.5kg (4½–5½lb), although can weigh up to 6.5kg (14lb). A related fish is the freshwater pike-perch or zander, which has the same two dorsal fins, but a more pike-like head. There is also a sea perch (*Serranus scriba*), a member of the Serranidae family, along with the sea bass and grouper.

Peculiarities Entirely carnivorous, eating larvae, worms, shrimps and own fry. Swim in shoals which diminish in size as they get older, thus the oldest perches may be solitary fish. The scales are deep seated and are easiest to remove immediately after the fish has been caught.

Where Found Still, fresh water of lakes and reservoirs, and slow-moving rivers throughout most of western Europe. They have been introduced to South Africa, New Zealand and Australia. Small perch occasionally seen in sandy bays.

Quality Delicate, lean and easily digested flesh. Care must be taken of bones.

Preparation Serve small perch whole and deep-fried. Fillet large fish and cook like carp. In Switzerland perch fillet (*Eglifilet*) is a speciality.

Pike
ESOX LUCIUS
Brochet

Brief Description Long roller-like bodies, mottled brown and green, with a single dorsal fin towards tail, a long jaw and a wide mouth of very sharp teeth; belly is whitish and fins red-brown. One species only in Europe, and several in North America. Best for the cook at 2–2.5kg (4½–5½lb), but the maximum is thought to be about 34kg (75lb).

Peculiarities A savage predator, and the fastest freshwater fish swimmer, the pike eats other fish, frogs, young birds and small mammals. A popular fish with anglers because it gives a good fight. Very slimy when caught.

Where Found Lakes, ponds, slow-moving rivers throughout northern hemisphere, both in Eurasia and America.

Quality Flesh is lean and firm with an excellent taste (larger fish can be a bit dry). Huge quantity of tiny soft disagreeable bones, vertical and fork-like. May have muddy taste, depending on diet and habitat. The liver is considered a delicacy.

Preparation Stuff small pike, cook whole, poach or braise. Bake slices and fillets. The flesh, especially of larger fish, is suitable for terrines and mousselines, and *quenelles de brochet* are world famous. Pike are particularly popular in Central Europe.

Plaice
PLEURONECTES PLATESSA
Carrelet, Plie-Franche

Brief Description   Saltwater, dextral flat fish, diamond shaped with rounded angles, and several bony knobs on its head. Grey or reddish brown with bright orange or red spots and white underside. Average length 30–40cm (12–16in) or less, though can grow to 75cm (30in); weighs 150–350g (5–12oz). The most commonly used flat fish in Britain.

Peculiarities   As with other bottom-lying fish, it feeds on small crustaceans, worms or molluscs. Hybrids with the flounder or dab have been found.

Where Found   North Sea, Atlantic coasts of Europe, and the Baltic. Occasionally found in west Mediterranean.

Quality   Lean, white, easily digested flesh; less delicate than sole.

Preparation   Grill or fry whole, bake fillets *en papillote*, sauté or poach and serve with sauces.

Common Prawn, Shrimp
PALAEMON SERRATUS
Crevette Rose

Brown Shrimp, Shrimp
CRANGON CRANGON
Crevette Grise

Brief Description   Of the lobster family. There are several varieties and sizes of prawn and their names in English are confusing: the British 'prawn' is the American 'shrimp' or 'jumbo shrimp'. Types most available are: common prawn (*Palaemon serratus*), pink, length up to 9cm (3½in); brown shrimp (*Crangon crangon*), same size, a semi-transparent grey when raw, brown when cooked; and the large red deep-sea prawn caught further north, *Pandalus borealis* (French: *crevette nordique*, English: King prawn), which is the one butterflied in restaurants.

Peculiarities   The smaller varieties are inshore, burrowing in sand and mud; they eat a huge variety of foodstuffs and are known as the principal scavengers of the ocean. The krill which whales eat – and the Japanese – are the smallest form of shrimp.

Where Found   Most shallow inshore waters, also in deeper waters in Atlantic and North Sea.

Quality   Varies according to variety, but they are best if bought or caught fresh. They go off quickly and are often frozen which can affect the quality.

Preparation   Usually available already cooked, but can be bought raw and quickly cooked, preferably in sea water. They can be deep-fried in a coating, or grilled on a skewer. Small shrimps caught on the west coast of Britain, particularly in Morecambe Bay, are potted with butter and mace, or eaten with buttered brown bread and lemon. Serve prawns in a variety of dishes and sauces to which they contribute colour and flavour.

Salmon, Atlantic Salmon
SALMO SALAR
Saumon

Brief Description   Salmon has an elongated body and small jutting jaw, and is grey-brown to light brown, to silver with black spots when adult, depending on age and location. It has a dark adipose fin characteristic of salmon family. Salmon spawn and live for the first two years in fresh water as brown and black spotted parr, when they are mere inches long. They migrate to sea water as smolts, when they become silvery in colour. Those that come back after one year are known as grilse: these measure about 50cm (20in) and can weigh up to 4kg (8¾lb). Those that come back after two, three or four years are adult salmon, and can weigh from 4–12kg (8¾–26½lb). There is also a Pacific salmon which belongs to a different genus, *Oncorhynchus*. Another less common genus of the salmon family is *Coregonus*, of which the pollan – a white fish resembling the herring – is a species.

Peculiarities   Salmon generally travel thousands of miles from their natal rivers to feed; feeding grounds of salmon from Europe and North America have been discovered off west Greenland, and others are north to the Faroes. When moving up river to spawn, salmon can leap up huge waterfalls (their name is derived from the Latin for leap). Most salmon die after spawning.

Where Found   In unpolluted and well oxygenated streams and rivers flowing into Atlantic and Pacific and Baltic and North Sea; and in those oceans and seas. Pollution and over fishing have decimated many salmon river populations.

Quality   Flesh of Atlantic salmon is pink, delicate, very nutritious and tasty, with creamy curd between the flakes; that of Pacific salmon is darker pink, and considered lesser in quality. Connoisseurs prefer salmon caught as it starts upstream, when it is fat and pink from feeding at sea. The flesh of the male is said to be more tender. Salmon are 'farmed' but they can lack flavour and the flesh is more flabby (possibly because their muscles are less exercised than those of the vigorously nomadic wild salmon).

Preparation   Poach and serve cold, or warm in delicate sauces. Grill as steaks. Make into mousses and terrines, use in pies, or bake wrapped in pastry. Smoked salmon is one of the world's greatest delicacies, as is the dill-marinated salmon, *gravlax*, of Scandinavia. Pacific salmon is canned (among the species used are Chinook, King, Coho, Sockeye and Chum), and the roe of the Keta or dog salmon is made into Keta, or red caviar.

Sardine

SARDINA PILCHARDUS

Sardine

Brief Description Small round sea fish similar to herring. Bluish green, with a white belly and two small spots on each side near the head. Large scales. Maximum length 20cm (8in), but smaller ones best to eat.

Peculiarities The sardine is an immature pilchard (this nomenclature does not apply in USA, where 'sardines' are a related but different species). Sardines live in vast shoals and are fished at night with lights.

Where Found Atlantic coasts from Canaries to South of Ireland, North Sea and as far as Norway in very hot summers, and in Mediterranean and Black Seas.

Quality Oily and aromatic, rich in iron and calcium. Best eaten fresh soon after being caught.

Preparation Grill or sauté. They were the first fish to be canned, in 1834. Connoisseurs claim that those grilled then matured in olive oil in cans for at least a year are best.

Scallop

PECTEN MAXIMUS

Coquille St Jacques

Brief Description Fan-shaped, vari-coloured marine bivalve mollusc, measuring up to 15cm (6in). Many varieties throughout the world: *P. maximus* is the Great scallop found in European waters, and the Mediterranean or Pilgrim scallop (*P. jacobaeus*) is a little smaller. The two types of scallop of commercial interest are the larger deep-sea scallop and the smaller bay scallop.

Peculiarities Scallops, unlike most bivalves, can swim by opening and closing their shells, using the white muscles – the part which is eaten.

Where Found Both sides of the Atlantic, the Mediterranean, but many species in many seas.

Quality The firmest-fleshed shellfish. Eat only the white muscle and the coral or roe (and the Americans discard the latter).

Preparation Cook *en brochette*, steam, sauté, poach, grill or deep-fry. Serve with a sauce, using the shells for dishes.

Scampi, Norway Lobster, Dublin Bay Prawn

NEPHROPS NORVEGICUS

Langoustine

Brief Description Smallest marine, lobster-like crustacean (apart from shrimps), measuring 12–15cm (5–6in), though it can achieve 25cm (10in). Pale rose with eight legs and two long claws (all white tipped). Does not change colour when cooked.

Peculiarities Creature has varying names in English language, including Dublin Bay prawn (it is prolific in the waters between the Isle of Man and the Irish coast) and scampi, the plural of the Italian name. Should not be confused with the freshwater crayfish (crawfish in the US, *écrevisse* in France).

Where Found East Atlantic, Adriatic and Mediterranean.

Quality Only the sweet, tender tails are eaten; better fresh than frozen.

Preparation Barbecue, poach, serve cold in salads or seafood platters, or hot in sauces. Best cooked alive. What is breadcrumbed, deep-fried and called scampi is not necessarily the Norway lobster . . .

Scorpion Fish

SCORPAENA SCROFA

Rascasse (Rouge), Scorpène

Brief Description Belongs to Scorpaemidae family and thus is related to the redfish, which it slightly resembles in shape. Red or orange, with an enormous head, and sharp, quite dangerous spines in the dorsal fins. Average length about 25cm (10in), but can reach 55cm (22in).

Peculiarities Many varieties of scorpion fish, three of them indigenous to the Mediterranean.

Where Found Mediterranean and in Atlantic up to Brittany. Varieties too in the West Atlantic, Pacific coasts of California and near New Zealand.

Quality Lean and tasty flesh. The liver is often considered a delicacy. Much waste when fish is cleaned because of large head, and some experts say that cheeks should be eaten.

Preparation A must for *bouillabaisse*. Large fish good stuffed and baked; or poach. Serve hot or cold.

Sea Bass

BICENTRARCHUS LABRAX

Bar, Loup de Mer

Brief Description Belongs to the family Serranidae, which includes sea perch and grouper. Slim and elegant fish; back is shiny, silver blue-grey, with two fins, the first of which has very sharp spines; the belly is white. The fish has strong scales. Average length 35–40cm (14–20in), but can reach 100cm (40in); weighs 50g–4kg (2oz–8¾lb), although they can be even larger. Expensive.

Peculiarities There are many other fish known as bass – salt and freshwater – but sea bass is most common, and most appreciated gastronomically.

Where Found   Sea, saltwater lakes, lower reaches of rivers; Mediterranean, Atlantic coast of Europe to Scandinavia; other varieties caught east coast America and south Atlantic.

Quality   One of the best white fish; firm, lean, flaky, very tasty flesh; delicate, easily bruised skin, and few bones.

Preparation   Poach or grill at low temperatures, steam, oven-braise, roast or bake, and serve with delicate sauces; holds its shape well when cooked.

Skate
RAJA DATIS

Pocheteau (Blanc), Raie

Brief Description   A member of the Rajidae family which includes the various rays; all are flattened sea fish. The skate is cartilaginous (non-bony), and kite-shaped, broad and flat with pectoral fins that have become wings; it has a long tail and snout (the latter distinguishes it from the ray), and grey or brown back with spots and dots. Grows to 2 metres (80in), and weighs up to 90kg (200lb).

Peculiarities   Triangular wings only are used in cooking (often thornback ray (*R. clacata*) wings are sold to be cooked in same way as skate). Both ray and skate have urea in their blood (required by cartilaginous fish to prevent them losing water from their tissue), which breaks up on death and smells strongly of ammonia. It disappears after 48 hours, and the flesh benefits from this time in cool storage. They sometimes catch their prey by enveloping it in their wings, and are said to be sensitive to music.

Where Found   Atlantic Ocean from Mediterranean to northern Norway, the Mediterranean, and related species in North American waters. Thornback ray ranges up to Iceland.

Quality   Skate usually sold as wings, often already skinned. Flesh is good quality: white and delicate, sometimes compared to crab. The liver is valued by some gourmets. Ray is lean and pale pink; less good than skate.

Preparation   May be prepared in a variety of ways, *raie au beurre noir* being the most famous. Bake, grill or poach (when the gelatinous bones will give a jelly), and eat hot or cold. Sauté small fish whole. Skate is popular in Britain in fish and chip shops.

Sole, Black Sole, Dover Sole
SOLEA SOLEA

Sole

Brief Description   There are several varieties of sole – the Sand or French sole, and the lemon sole or *limande*

(which *isn't* actually a sole, but a member of the plaice family) – but the one acknowledged to be the best is the Common, Black or Dover sole. A marine, dextral flat fish, it is an elongated oval almost completely surrounded by fins; grey to grey-brown, white on the blind side. Maximum length about 50cm (20in); weighs from 175–300g (6–10oz).

Peculiarities   Top side of sole, like most flat fish, changes colour according to surroundings (this is the reason for its occasional irregular black markings when alive). The sole is attributed to Dover simply because that port was once the best and quickest supplier to London of freshly caught sole.

Where Found   Mediterranean, Atlantic (not on west side), English Channel, and North Sea up to Scotland and southern Norway.

Quality   Delicate, lean, easily digestible and tasty flesh. Other soles are much less good. The quality depends on the provenance.

Preparation   Poach, sauté, grill, bake, or stuff. The fillets are very easy to roll (keep skin side inside).

Squid
LOLIGO FORBESI, LOLIGO VULGARIS

Encornet, Calmar

Brief Description   Slim cephalopod with large eyes; torpedo-shaped body with two broad triangular shaped fins at one end, a cluster of ten tentacles at the other. Ivory coloured, often with a violet spotted membrane; maximum body length is 60cm (24in), although usually sold smaller (the smaller the better). Several varieties of edible squid, but two most common are *L. forbesi* and *L. vulgaris*. The squid is most numerous of the cephalopods, and highly prized as food, especially in Japan.

Peculiarities   If disturbed, its body can very rapidly blush a brownish colour. They are fished at night with lights in the Mediterranean. Squid are surface swimmers – almost transparent and invisible to predators. They swim strongly by jetting water through their bodies.

Where Found   *L. forbesi*: north-east Atlantic as far south as the UK; *L. vulgaris*: further south and in the Mediterranean. Other varieties found throughout the world.

Quality   Tentacles are most delicate part; larger squid require prolonged cooking, but smaller ones, with bodies less than 75cm (3in) long, can be chopped into rings and quick fried. Squid over 15cm (6in) long in the body can be stuffed.

Preparation   Stuff, grill, sauté, deep-fry, stew and use in salads. They are dried in China. All cephalopods – squid, cuttlefish and octopus – contain ink sacs which can be used in various ways, and *calamar en su tinta* (in its ink) is a Spanish speciality.

Swordfish
XIPHIAS GLADIUS
Espadon

Brief Description Largest round bony sea fish. Dark back, silver-white belly and long sharp sword which accounts for a third of maximum length 5 metres (166 feet), when it could weigh 500kg (over 1000lb). Generally landed much smaller: about 70–100kg (155–222lb).

Peculiarities Probably fastest of all fish (can reach about 100km (60 miles) per hour). A solitary, deep-water, oceanic fish, normally caught by harpoon. Can ram with its sword, which was often embedded in ships' wooden hulls, but more usual to stun prey (fish or cephalopods) sideways.

Where Found Atlantic, west and east, Mediterranean and Black Sea, and world wide in tropical and temperate seas.

Quality White, firm, fine-grained; aromatic and meaty. One bone only down the back.

Preparation Grill or bake the steaks – which can be up to 30cm (12in) in diameter – or grill *en brochette*. Swordfish is smoked in Turkey and Portugal.

Trout
SALMO TRUTTA
Truite

Brief Description There are two main types of trout native to northern Europe: brown trout (completely freshwater), and sea trout (spends part of its life in the sea, and spawns in fresh water). There are many subspecies of brown trout (*Salmo trutta fario*) throughout the world but principal division is into trout of river or of lake. Brown trout are, in general, long and shapely, silvery grey, occasionally golden brown, with black, sometimes red, spots on the back, and a black-brown tail. Size ranges from tiny fish which are thrown back by anglers to giants of up to 10kg (20lb). Colouration and size depend on diet and habitat.

Rainbow trout (*Salmo gairdneri*) are similar to brown trout in shape, have a pinkish or rainbow band along their silver spotted sides, and dorsal fin and tail liberally sprinkled with black spots. They were introduced from California in 1882 and now occur world wide.

Peculiarities The lake trout often goes into moving water to spawn; the river trout will swim up river to selected spawning areas. The rainbow trout, which can exist in warmer and less pure water than any of the brown trout, and are thus much more adaptable, are stocked in small lakes and reservoirs formerly suitable only for coarse fish, and they are the variety found in trout farms.

Where Found Brown trout: pure streams, rivers and lakes throughout Europe and parts of Asia, and in North America. Rainbow trout: native to both sides of the Pacific, found in lakes, streams and rivers – and often in the sea where it feeds – and have been introduced to Australasia, South America, Africa, Europe, and South Asia.

Quality Brown trout have a delicate white flesh, easily digested and nutty in flavour. Bones easily removed. Lake trout are thought to be less flavourful than river, and can often be drier. Farmed trout too can lack flavour.

Preparation Cook 'bleu', poach, sauté, grill, steam or bake. They are good cold. Both brown and rainbow can be smoked, but it is the latter which is normally used.

Sea Trout, Salmon Trout
SALMO TRUTTA TRUTTA
Truite de Mer, Truite Saumonée

Brief Description A larger, sea-going variety of common or brown trout; difficult to distinguish from salmon for the layman, but in general are silvery white with dark spotted backs. They can become redder or darker at spawning time, when they might be difficult to distinguish from brown trout. Vary in size according to age: 500g–1kg (1–2lb) at one year, up to 4kg (8¾lb) a year later. They can grow, in certain seas like the Baltic, up to 13.5kg (30lb).

Peculiarities Commonly called salmon trout because of pink flesh, caused in the wild by its diet of marine crustaceans; when reared in fisheries this colour can be induced by artificial means. Like salmon, returns to its natal river to spawn but does not make such long journeys from its territorial waters as the salmon.

Where Found Fast-flowing and clean rivers throughout Europe, in the Baltic and the North Atlantic, from North Africa to Iceland. Runs of sea trout have been established in Tierra del Fuego, the Falklands, and Tasmania. They are farmed in Norway, Denmark and the USA.

Quality Very fine, oily flesh, more delicate and slightly paler than salmon.

Preparation As for salmon or trout.

Tuna
THUNNUS THYNNUS
Thon (Rouge), Germon

Brief Description Largest members of mackerel family, Scombridae. Best known of several tuna species are blue-fin tuna (*T. thynnus*) and long-fin tuna or Albacore (*T. alalunga*). Both have spindle-shaped bodies, dark blue backs, silver-grey sides and belly.

The blue-fin can reach length of 4 metres (13 feet) but more normally about 1–2 metres (3½–6 feet); the long-fin is smaller, 1 metre (3½ feet) at most. The Atlantic and Pacific bonitos are members of same family.

Peculiarities Predators, who are themselves taken by killer whales and, primarily, by man. They swim in schools, but schools are size related, and the largest may be solitary.

Where Found Warm waters world wide: the blue-fin in Atlantic north to Iceland, and in Mediterranean and Black Sea; long-fin also in Pacific.

Quality Blue-fin has dark, close-texured, oily flesh, rich in vitamins. The cuts are like meat, are highly prized and eaten raw by the Japanese. Long-fin has whiter, less heavy flesh, which changes to pink during cooking. The belly is the most valued part in Spain and Italy, and is called *ventresca.*

Preparation Braise, grill or bake *en papillote. Botargo* or *boutargue* is made from the female roes.

Turbot
SCOPHTHALMUS MAXIMUS
Turbot, Turbotia

Brief Description Lozenge-shaped sinistral flat fish, sandy brown to yellowish grey (depending on sea floor colouration), with black and white spots; its dark sides rather warty. Adults measure generally 40–50cm (16–20in) and can weigh up to 20kg (45lb); baby or chicken turbot (*turbotin*) are very much smaller, about 1–2kg (2¾–4½lb).

Peculiarities Known as the pheasant of the sea to the Romans, the Italians still refer to it as *il fagiano del mare.* Occasionally hybrids with brill occur.

Where Found European waters only, in the Mediterranean, in the Atlantic to Iceland, and in the North, Baltic and Mediterranean Seas.

Quality Excellent, very tasty firm white flesh, which many consider second only to Dover sole. Bones rich in gelatine which makes the flesh succulent and gives body to sauces made with the poaching liquid.

Preparation Braise in oven or poach, whole or filleted; grill or sauté fillets or steaks.

Whiting
MERLANGIUS MERLANGUS
Merlan

Brief Description Small, long round sea fish of cod family. Dark blue or green back, with silver or white sides and belly. Has a black mark on each side and no barbels, a feature of many of the family. Average length 30cm (12in); weight 150–200g (5–7oz).

Peculiarities The young, with the young of the haddock and the horse mackerel, often take protection from predators by staying close to jellyfish. A voracious predator itself, it lives off crustaceans and smaller fish.

Where Found Shallow inshore waters of Atlantic Ocean as far as Iceland, in English Channel, Mediterranean, Black and Baltic Seas. Very common in North Sea.

Quality Very white, good, tender flesh, which can be dryish, so needs to be prepared with care. Easily digested, so may be used for invalids. Must not be squashed during transport; head is particularly vulnerable. The delicate flesh deteriorates rapidly.

Preparation Deep-fry, stuff, poach and serve with sauces. Can be smoked, and it is dried in Scotland.

Glossary of Terms, Techniques and Ingredients

Al dente Usually applied to vegetables and pasta that are slightly undercooked so that they are crunchy or have some resistance to the bite.

Bain-marie A roasting or baking tray half-filled with hot water in which terrines, custards, sauces, etc., stand to cook, usually in the oven. The food is protected from fierce direct heat, and poaches in a gentle steamy atmosphere. It is also used for keeping foods warm and waiting, without the contents being spoiled by overheating or dryness. A double-boiler on top of the stove serves a similar purpose.

Baste To spoon hot fat or liquid over food being roasted, baked or poached in the oven in order to keep the food moist and juicy and prevent it drying out.

Blanch Either to bring food rapidly from cold to boiling point in water and boil for a very short time, or to add food to hot water to close the pores and retain colour and nutrients. After boiling plunge briefly into ice-cold water to refresh (see below). Blanching also removes strong flavours from some foods, and the shells or skins from others.

Bouquet garni Contributes flavour to foods. Can be changed according to needs of recipe, but usually a mixture of parsley stalks, bay leaf, peppercorns and thyme wrapped with celeriac and carrots, and tied together. A white bouquet garni consists only of onion, white of leek and celeriac plus herbs. It is used for white stocks.

Brunoise A garnish, like julienne, where the vegetables are cut into the smallest possible dice.

Butter Butter is one of the best cooking mediums for fish – mainly because of its flavour – but it must be unsalted. It is ideal for sautéing, or basting fish while grilling. Salted butters brown and burn at a lower temperature than unsalted, so the food discolours too. Salted butter can also make foods stick to the pan. Clarified butter – butter from which the milk solids, salt and liquid are separated out, leaving a clear fat – has the highest burning point.

To clarify 100g (¼lb) butter, heat gently in a pan until there is foam on the top. Simmer for another 3–5 minutes – do not allow to brown – then skim well and pour off into a bowl, ideally through muslin. Any solids still left will sink to the bottom of the bowl to be scraped off the solid butter when set. There will be about 50–75g (2–3oz).

Coulis A thick liquid purée of fruit or vegetables, usually tomatoes, made without flour.

Court bouillon A seasoned liquid or stock in which to poach fish or shellfish.

Deglaze To add liquid – wine, stock, water or cream – to a frying pan, saucepan or roasting tin in which food has been roasted or sautéed after the fat has been poured off. The liquid is gently heated and the tasty particles, juices and sediments stuck to the base and sides of the pan are scraped and stirred into the liquid to make a gravy or sauce or the basis of either.

Dorsal fin One or several fins situated in a line along the back of a round fish; there may be a fleshy dorsal fin (an adipose fin) near the tail.

Émincer To cut into small slices.

Escalope A thin slice of flesh, usually veal, but which is applied to some fish cuts as well, for example salmon.

Fillet A prime cut of fish, with all bones removed.

Garnish An edible decoration added to savoury and sweet dishes to improve appearance, to awaken tastes, and to add variety, texture or colour. For instance, roe of all kinds – of the sturgeon (caviar), salmon and lobster – are used with fish as colourful and tasty garnishes.

Gelatine Leaf gelatine is used in a few recipes throughout the book, and should this be unavailable, use gelatine powder instead. One leaf weighs about 2g (just over ⅛oz), so use the equivalent weight of powder.

Glaze To add a gloss, and thereby enhance the appearance of food. For savoury dishes, brush with a thin layer of reduced meat, poultry or fish stock, for pastries or bread use milk or beaten egg and for vegetables toss in a reduction of stock or juices.

Julienne Usually vegetables or citrus rind cut into long thin strands like matchsticks, not longer than the width of a soup spoon.

Lard Usually to thread strips of fat through meat which has no natural marbling of fat. In the case of fish for braising – such as tuna or swordfish – larding with anchovies is for additional flavour rather than for additional moisture. With a small sharp knife, make an incision and insert an anchovy fillet, half or whole. Do this evenly across one side of the piece or steak of fish.

Marinade A seasoned liquid in which to soak fish before further preparation to give flavour and to tenderise.

Medallions Small rounds of fish or shellfish, evenly cut. A *mignon* is similar.

Olive oil Olive oils vary enormously, and the best to use with fish are cold pressed: these are the pure virgin oils made by one simple pressing, with nothing else added. (They are further classified according to acidity.) Any residues from this first pressing are hot water or steam treated, then pressed again and used as a blend for cheaper, less flavourful olive oils.

Oven temperatures The following are roughly equivalent oven dial markings, not exact conversions.

Description	Degrees Celsius	Degrees Fahrenheit	Gas Mark
Very cool	110	225	¼
	120	250	½
Cool	140	275	1
	150	300	2
Moderate	160	325	3
	180	350	4
Moderately hot	190	375	5
	200	400	6
Hot	220	425	7
	230	450	8
Very hot	240	475	9

en papillote Literally, an envelope. A wrapping of paper or foil in which fish is baked to contain aroma, flavour and moisture.

Quenelles Most commonly, a light mousseline mixture of finely minced fish with cream, which is poached like a dumpling. A quenelle should be shaped like an egg between two warm wet tablespoons, and then slid into simmering liquid to poach.

Reduce Literally to reduce the quantity of a liquid by boiling in a shallow uncovered pan in order to concentrate the liquid and its flavour. Stocks and wines should be boiled rapidly; cream less rapidly, otherwise it boils over, and burns on the side of the pan.

Refresh To plunge into ice-cold water, or to hold briefly under running cold water to stop the cooking process. This is usually done to vegetables after boiling or blanching, to set the colour.

Slake To mix a non-soluble powder, eg cornflour, with a little cold liquid to a thin paste which can then be added to a sauce to thicken it if necessary.

Warm, to keep Fish should be cooked as late as possible and served as soon as possible. If fish has to be kept warm while a sauce is finished, keep in a low oven, but do not cover, as the flesh will soften in the trapped steam.

To keep a sauce warm, place in the top half of a double boiler over warm water, or in a container in a bain-marie holding warm water. This applies particularly to the butter-based sauces which can separate or curdle if too high a heat is applied. If the sauce is likely to form a skin, cover tightly with a butter paper or greased greaseproof paper, or cover the container with pierced cling film.

Yoghurt Yoghurt is formed from cow's, sheep's or goat's milk by the addition and action of benevolent bacilli. It is digested more rapidly and easily than raw milk, and its mild acidity is good for the stomach. It is a satisfying food, and is low in calories, especially when made with skimmed milk.

Index